THE VICTORY OF HOPE

The Victory of Hope

A JOURNEY

FROM GOOD FRIDAY

TO EASTER

Michael Kitchener

First published in Great Britain 1994
Society for Promoting Christian Knowledge
Holy Trinity Church
Marylebone Road
London NW1 4DU

British Library Cataloguing-in-Publication Data
A catalogue record for this book is available from the British Library

ISBN 0–281–04731–6

Typeset by Datix International, Bungay, Suffolk

Printed and bound in Great Britain by
BPCC Paperbacks Ltd
Member of BPCC Ltd

Contents

PART ONE

Good Friday

1 · The Human Pilgrimage – *City of Destruction*

Every story, so we are told, has a beginning, a middle and an end. For each of us, our own story had its beginning (according to different points of view) either when we were born, or when we were conceived, or at some point between those two events. Our conscious story, the life of which we are openly aware, begins a little later, with the earliest memories which we can call to mind. And it ends, as far as our story in this world is concerned, with our death; or so at any rate we assume. We can at least say this, that there will be a time when we no longer have the sort of life which we know within this world, whatever other sort of life we may or may not then enjoy.

So our story is defined within those two points, our beginning and our end. All that lies between them is the middle. But our beginning is for us now no more than memory; and everything else that was once our immediate experience has passed with our beginning into memory, too. Our end is as yet only expectation, whether expected with hope or with fear; and everything else that will one day be our immediate experience is at this moment only expectation, too.

So we live between memory and expectation, and the tiny moment of our living present moves on its journey between these two. Nor can we pick up our own story like a book and return to live again its earlier pages or cheat on expectation by turning ahead to see what happens at the end. We are imprisoned in the narrow space of every present moment as it comes, and the vast bulk of our life is at one remove from our experience now, disappeared already into memory or still shrouded in the cloud of future expectation.

Some have said that this imprisonment in the present is responsible for most of human pain. The pain of regret, as we look back on things which we would have done differently, but now we cannot change. The pain of shame, as moments which we would rather not remember at all recall themselves with an inward shudder to our mind. The pain of guilt, as we remember relationships broken or marred through our neglect or cruelty, hopes once enjoyed now dashed to the ground and never to be restored. Or else the pain of longing, as we remember days of joy and innocence, moments of beauty, times of peace and friendship, simple contentment in God's world; all past and gone, beyond recapture or the hope of repetition. All these kinds of pain come from the fact that the past is now no more than memory, and will not return.

Expectation has its pain as well. There is the pain of fear, ranging from mild apprehension through every degree to heart-chilling dread of that which we know to be a possibility but try to keep away from our awareness. But there is also a pain involved in hope, as we yearn for something to happen and in that yearning dread the possibility that it will not; or as in our eager looking forward we find we have no heart to address the demands which the present makes on us, and maybe miss some crucial challenge. Such pains as these are derived from our expectation of the future which is not yet with us but is coming.

There are several ways in which we may try to escape these pains. One is simply by shutting our eyes to them, and resting complacently in the belief that all is well and straightforward. The naïve belief in progress was once a widespread expression in our society of that idea; but that belief is harder for us now to maintain, after all that our century has experienced and with all the terrors which our age still fears. We can quickly look around us and see justice in the traditional Christian claim that human life is somehow fatally handicapped in moral terms, and there is no building of paradise here on earth by us; the problems are too unmanageable, the issues too complicated, and humanity does not, it seems, learn much from experience. Complacency about our world is not perhaps a great temptation just at present.

So maybe we fall into a second way, the way of social and political despair. Short of a wholesale overturning of the present way of things – what in political terms is called a 'revolution' – the oppressed peoples of the world are not going to be released from their slavery, the bitterness at the heart of Northern Ireland is not going to ease, the number of young people in our country who go straight from school to permanent unemployment is not going to be cut drastically, there is not going to be any world-wide redistribution of the resources of food and energy on which we all depend. Those who think otherwise, who suppose that reason, humanity and moderation will succeed in the world of public and international affairs, are liable to be dismissed as unrealistic, misty-eyed fools (at best) or denounced (at worst) as cynical exploiters of a popular but impossible dream.

We can easily see the same dark picture in our own lives, too. If we have reached any measure at all of self-awareness, how can we fail to notice the absence of progress in combatting our besetting sins? How time after time we search our conscience and recognize the same old faults, year after year we make the same resolutions and fail in more or less the same old way? Here too, perhaps, we begin to lose hope. We confess our sins to God, and we ask for God's grace to amend our lives; yet with little expectation in our hearts that it will be so, little belief that this time it will be any different.

And all of this, perhaps, we put down to the weakness of our condition. If our way were only smooth, if we were only free to advance along the path of goodness we intend! But no; we are (as the theologians say) 'fallen', our own strength and even our desires are fatally impaired by the sinful condition of all humanity. If only it were never necessary in the political and economic life of the world to achieve one person's good at another's expense, if only all could equally have all their good fulfilled together! But no; we are 'fallen', trapped in all sorts of morally intolerable situations; from the waging of wars for justice and freedom's sake to the aborting of unborn babies for the health and safety of their mothers; from the inhuman treatment of criminals in our prisons for the protection of society to the inhumane treatment of animals in factory farms to provide us with essential food. It is very sad, it is extremely regrettable, but not in the last resort (we tell ourselves) our fault; it is how things are in this imperfect world, the inevitable consequence of the Fall.

It is indeed a truth affirmed in the Christian tradition that we are fallen, bound up in the sinfulness of all humanity from its beginnings. Yet to excuse ourselves from our own responsibility because of this is to abuse that truth, and our doing it is one symptom of our fallen condition. In the ancient story in which the truth of our fallenness is most familiarly expressed, the story of Adam and Eve, one of the first outcomes of their sin is their shifting the blame away from themselves. Adam abuses Eve's disobedience and Eve the serpent's temptation when they use them as excuses for evading their own responsibility; this even though the serpent did tempt her, and she did in her turn tempt her husband. There are in the same way truths about ourselves which we are tempted to use as excuses. For example, one of the things which the traditional doctrine of the Fall seeks to keep before our minds is our human solidarity, the fact that we are all involved in a world together, conditioned by our past. There is a real sense in which we are trapped by what has made us what we are, graphically expressed in St Paul's phrase, 'All die in Adam' (1 Cor. 15.22). The evils that we do are indeed things which, if not exactly forced upon us, are yet urged on us by the nature of our existence. The past weighs down upon us; not only our own personal past, the mistakes which we ourselves have made and the sins we personally have committed, though their burden can be heavy enough; not only our communal past, the sins of our society, our civilization, and our church too which now limit the options open to us and cannot be shaken off at will; not only these but the past of humanity itself, the turmoil of evolutionary conflict out of which we came and which made us the kind of animals we are. All that is true, and yet to use its truth to evade our own responsibility is to be blind to a further truth about ourselves, which is that we are called to be more than just our past. To take refuge in excuses is to take refuge in despair about ourselves, and despair as much as complacency is a form of blindness to the truth.

Other forms of escape from our pain are more assertive, taking matters into our hands to remedy our situation. We know that there are not grounds for complacency, and we are aware of the trap of despair. So perhaps we seek to prevent the present from slipping into the past, hanging onto those good things which we now enjoy and building round them a cage of changelessness.

The biblical myth of Babel depicts with ironic clarity this human tendency. In that ancient tale, humanity begins in unity and is motivated by fear of losing it. Humanity seeks to cling to that present good by building a tower to 'make a name for ourselves, so that we do not get scattered all over the world' (Gen. 11.4). But real life does not allow us to stand still in the present. As so often in the Bible, God in the story of Babel represents reality; and reality steps into the human dream. Reality decrees that we shall move on; and the very attempt which we make to hold on to the present becomes the cause of our downfall, precipitates our moving on. Precisely because of the tower which they had attempted to build, their worst fear was realized when the Lord 'scattered them thence all over the world, and they stopped building the city' (Gen. 11.8). We cannot eliminate the passing of present into past, for reality all around us is changing whether we decide to go with it or not. If we try to resist that passage of time by clinging to what is now past as if it were still present, we shall find ourselves isolated, cut off from reality and from other people, and the present which once we truly enjoyed will be enjoyable no more.

Another way in which we may try to escape by assertion the pains with which the passage of time surrounds us is in seeking to eliminate hope and fear by reaching forward to grasp for ourselves that future which we desire to come. The story of Eden provides the classical biblical expression of this. The knowledge of good and evil, which the man and the woman are forbidden to take, is not moral discernment, the ability to see what is right and wrong. They must have that already, or there would be no point in God's giving them a commandment at all. The forbidden knowledge which they seize by eating the fruit is, rather, the ability to decide for themselves what is right and what is wrong, that divine knowledge of the principles of reality which God alone has because God knows all possibilities, outside the limitation of the passage of time. We are set in the garden of God's creation as stewards to tend it, to bring its fruit to perfection; it is not given to us to step outside that role. The eating of the forbidden fruit is the attempt to be 'like God', to escape the uncertainties of hope and fear, to become the masters of our own destiny and no longer servants of our Creator. That attempt also is doomed to failure. Ultimately, the man and the woman are expelled from the garden; their world is no longer a paradise, but a place of hard labour and trouble. Just as humanity at Babel is shown as forfeiting our blessings by the very attempt to cling on to them, so humanity in Eden is shown as descending below our natural condition by our attempt to rise above it, entering a life of deep apprehension by our attempt to set ourselves beyond it.

Nor is this tragic outcome merely some sort of divine revenge taken on us for daring to usurp God's prerogative. The fall of humanity into something less than we are meant to be is represented in this myth as the natural and immediate outcome of our stepping outside the boundaries of our existence. They eat the fruit, and immediately the knowledge which the serpent promised is theirs. They stand outside their condition, observing themselves as it were from above, and what they see in this new-found self-consciousness is that they are naked, and that vision brings them shame. So they are cut off from God, driven into hiding from that divine wisdom which also knows their nakedness. As the story progresses, we discover how they are also cut off from each other, and from the rest of God's creatures. The man blames the woman for his sin, the woman blames the serpent; their action has brought bitterness and enmity into the world, and the divine sentence of expulsion is but reality's confirmation of that which they already experience in themselves.

There is a very ancient Christian way of reading this myth of our condition, in which a distinction is made between God's image and God's likeness. 'Let us make man', says God, 'in our image, after our likeness.' We are made, it is suggested, as essentially beings who are on a journey. The goal of our journey, the promise held out to us, is to grow into the likeness of God. 'We know that when Christ appears', says St John (1 John 3.2), 'we shall be like him, for we shall see him as he is.' That is our future. The image of God is our present, the potential for love which is even now given to us, through which we are able to grow into God's likeness. Our sin, as expressed in the story of Adam and Eve, is to seize prematurely the future to which we must move. In that act of taking what is not yet given to us we refuse what is given, the potential to grow.

So both these assertive avenues of escape from the pain of the passage of time lead us out of movement and growth into stagnation and death. Both avenues are linked, for both are aspects of one and the same basic fault, which is the sin both of Adam and of Babel; and that is the fault of supposing that here and now, in this present moment, we can decide for ourselves the people we are to be. The way of clinging to the present when it should be allowed to become the past is an attempt to say, 'This is where I will stay; I am satisfied with this, and I will not move from here to another state.' The way of grasping at the future before it has arrived says, 'That is what I have decided it will be good for me to become; that is the ideal I choose, and I secure it now before circumstances can take it away.'

Jesus is represented by the Gospels as reserving his most stringent rebukes for the Pharisees, those good and righteous men of first-century Israel. Our Gospel writers often have him levelling against them the criticism of hypocrisy; but hypocrisy in the way that we normally understand it was not in fact a just charge to bring against the Pharisees. They were not in general shallow in their religion, professing one thing while doing another. We can better identify the true cause of Jesus' strictures against them by considering one of the best known examples of those strictures, the parable of the Pharisee and the publican who went into the temple to pray. The publican, he says, 'went home justified; the other did not' (Luke 18.14).

The Pharisee was justifiably proud of his achievement. He had done all the good things and had avoided all the sins which he listed; he was not lying before God about that. But his prayer was not genuinely prayer to God, but rather prayer 'to himself' (Luke 18.11). He was enclosed within his own ideal, his own image of himself, and in that enclosure was so cut off from humanity that he could even thank God that he was not like other people. He did all that the Law commanded, and more; his doubling of the regular weekly fast practised by devout Jews, and his scrupulous payment of tithes of every single item he received, went beyond the demands of the Law as received from God. That fact is the clue to the Pharisee's real sin. He had decided what sort of man he wished to be, and the measure of his fault was that he had succeeded. He had grasped his future already for himself, and was now intent on retaining it without change for ever. He was creating for himself a tradition of supposed holiness, the same kind of tradition which Jesus attacked on other occasions because it interfered with true obedience to the demands of life in obedience to God (see especially Mark 7.1–13).

It comes as a shock to humanity to be told that our goodness has the nature of sin, but that is the clear teaching of the Scriptures, so long as our goodness comes from our own decisions about what is right and wrong, and not from obedience to God. Our righteousness turns out to have the same effect as despair after all; it is a barrier to God's will for us, so long as it reflects our desire to escape from the journey of time from the remembered past into the expected future, our desire to stand still and hold on to a sure achievement of our own. In the early years of the fourteenth century, the Italian poet Dante wrote *The Divine Comedy*, a work which remains one of the greatest pieces of literature in the world, and one of the most profound explorations of our human pilgrimage. To three aspects of that pilgrimage the three parts of the poem, Hell, Purgatory and Heaven, correspond.

At the beginning of the first part, Dante finds himself in the middle of life, and in a dark wood of perplexity, moral and spiritual confusion and doubt. He is led out of this state by being shown in succession the state of those who are lost for ever to God's love, the state of those who are on their way to God, and the state of those who enjoy the vision and love of God eternally. He descends in hell by a downward spiral into the very centre of the earth. As he goes, he meets sinners of every kind, both small and great. The one thing which unites them all is that they did not in life repent of their sins; content with the way they were, they decided to remain in the state which they had chosen for themselves. Their eternal punishment is nothing less than being allowed to enjoy the fruits of their decision. They remain for ever fixed in hell in those besetting sins which they had decided not to forgo. The lustful are imprisoned in eternal embrace, the angry in eternal wrath, the indolent in eternal torpor. At the centre and the bottom-most point of hell, the mouth to which the whole funnel-like structure tends, is Satan himself, the epitome of rebellious pride. He was once, so the myth has it, the most beautiful of all God's angels, Lucifer 'The Bearer of Light'. But Lucifer was not content to be God's servant, he had to seize his destiny for himself. So by himself he exists in the absolute cold of self-contemplating pride, eternally devouring the most terrible of the sinners in his kingdom as pride devours us when we make ourselves its subjects by refusing our obedience to God.

The complacency which rests on our own human achievements as if they were unambiguously good; the despair which accepts the evil in our present condition and says things will never be different – we are fated to be like the beasts, for we are only a complex kind of animal, after all; the self-directing assertiveness of Babel and Adam and the Pharisee, by which we exert ourselves in our own will to escape from our predicament: all have in common the absence of one critical virtue, patient hope. Complacency rejects hope, for it thinks there is no need to be different from the way we are. Despair rejects hope, for it thinks there is no other condition to which we poor beasts might be called. Self-directing assertiveness rejects hope too, for it thinks that even as we are now we can reach out and take all the good things we may ever want, as we are now we can make a better world than our ancestors did, as we are now we can evade the evils with which we are beset.

Against all these hope-denying attitudes, hope is an always forward-looking yearning and expectancy of things which are not yet as they shall be. Hope insists that where we are now is no resting place but only the beginning of a journey. There is a journey to undertake, we are not to rest complacently or despairingly with the present way of things. The journey is yet to be undertaken; we have not yet reached its goal and so we cannot yet with safety seize upon its fruit. Our human tragedy is that we cannot seem to break free of one or other of the false and hope-denying ways.

Through me you go to the city of sorrow;
through me you go to the eternal pain;
through me you go among the race of the lost.

Justice moved my high Creator;
by the divine Power I was made,
by supreme Wisdom and primordial Love.

Before me were no things created
except the eternal, and I last for eternity myself;
abandon all hope, you who enter me.

Dante Alighieri
The Divine Comedy, 'Hell' Book I, Canto 3
[translated by Michael Kitchener]

That is the inscription written over the door which leads to hell. We live between memory and expectation. There is no escape from that except into the self-absorbed deadness of hell; and that means hell on earth, no less than the dreadful possibility that we may become so fixed in our own wilfulness on earth that we cannot escape from it even when we die. To abandon that painful acceptance of change, that painful acceptance of the fact that we are always moving into an unknown future, is to abandon hope, for it is only on the foundation of memory and expectation that hope is built.

2 · THE CRUCIFIED – *FAILURE*

WE SHALL NEVER approach the truth of the cross, until we have grasped the profound degree to which it is a failure and a sharing in the frustration of our fallen condition. Jesus did not desire to do it this way; he pleaded in Gethsemane that some other path might be found, and his pleadings failed. If that was his view of it in Gethsemane, can it have been wholly different before? Should we in fact have any respect for him if we thought he had gone eagerly to his death, not as the only way open to him but positively as the thing which he had always desired?

Consider the failures which bring him to Calvary. There are of course the well-known failures: the failure of Pilate to preserve that justice for which as governor he stands; the failure of Caiaphas to yield to the Messiah sent by the God he serves; the failure of Peter to meet his proud boasts of undying loyalty. Yes, in the passion of Jesus every human agency, every earthly power is tried and found wanting. The self-directing assertiveness of human pride suffers a death-blow. All that is true; but we must consider his own failure, too.

The Gospels speak of him as 'teacher'. The place where we go to judge the success of a teacher is to the understanding built up in the pupils. What understanding has Jesus succeeded in fostering even in his closest disciples, who on the very eve of his passion have been squabbling with each other about precedence and importance? How far has this teacher succeeded, who preached the sermon on the mount and now at his arrest has seen his disciples react to hostility not by 'turning the other cheek' but either by striking out with the sword or by running away?

The Gospels present him as a prophet, with the most critically important prophetic message ever to have been delivered. Where has he succeeded in this? Those by whom he must make himself heard – the priests and other religious leaders of God's people – these he has alienated completely, set at enmity with himself. Can we entirely blame them for their hostility? His sometimes harsh and extreme language has hardly been calculated to put them in a frame of mind to listen to him; his repeated neglect of Sabbath and purity observances has been hard to understand as anything but anti-social irresponsibility. These customs were not, for Jews of that period, simply petty regulations dreamed up by religious bureaucrats to make life hard. The strict keeping of the Sabbath, and strict segregation of the clean from the unclean, those within the Law from those outside it, had been the salvation of the Jewish people under pressure time and again for centuries. They were by now among the foundations of their social fabric; and you do not, if you are a responsible person, demolish such foundations without offering something pretty adequate in their place.

Jesus has played havoc with the fabric of Jewish society without offering any such concrete alternative. That is his trouble. He has knowingly or unknowingly got himself involved in political conflict, and now he must pay the price. Caiaphas, according to one account, has sealed the fate of Jesus with the political judgement, 'It is to your advantage that one man should die for the people, rather than that the whole nation should perish'

(John 11.50). Within the terms of realistic politics, Caiaphas is right: if Jesus is allowed to go on, their society will be in uproar, the Romans will sooner or later step in with force to sort things out as they have done so often before; and that could be the end of Jewish national identity. Getting rid of Jesus is, in realistic political terms, no more than giving him what he deserves for meddling in areas where he does not have the muscle – or apparently the will – to take control.

But perhaps his greatest failure is with Judas. Here he has failed not only himself and his mission, but his friend too. He has allowed Judas to slip into his dreadful sin; more than that, he has put temptation into Judas' way by calling him into dangerously close association with himself. Given Judas' sinful potential, and given what we are told of Jesus' insight into people's hearts, was it the act of a responsible leader to choose him as an Apostle? Was it fair to Judas, as the darker side of his character began to emerge, to allow him to carry on and not dismiss him even at the eleventh hour? When those who are involved in ordination training see someone go forward to ordination who before long falls disastrously from grace, they take it as a reflection on themselves that they were either not wise enough to notice the danger-signals in time or else not brave enough to act upon them. Should we not expect at least as much from Jesus?

So he hangs on his cross, a failed teacher, failed prophet, failed Messiah, failed friend. This surely must have been a large part of his agony in Gethsemane. Not a simple fear of death; there have been countless martyrs who have gone courageously to their deaths without such torment. But, rather, an unwillingness that this should be the end of the road, because he knew how much he had yet to achieve, how his work had not even begun. If only he could have more time! But no; events march inexorably on, and his future is taken out of his control. Now for him there is no future, no hope, no God. 'My God, my God, why have you forsaken me?' (Mark 15.34). He has even failed to achieve a permanent resolution of his own inner struggle; that cry from the cross is the agony of Gethsemane not permanently resolved but breaking out again at the last hour.

Thus Jesus is reduced to the failed plaything of circumstances, a tattered sign in flesh and blood nailed up to a wooden post as a warning to passers-by, suffering a death whose purpose was to dehumanize its victims in the act of getting rid of them. The watchers jeer at his helplessness: 'Come down from the cross, if you can!' Of course, he cannot. His real humanity prevents him from taking that way of escape from his condition; but it saves him from the sin of evading his cross only by removing any future he might have at all. In objective, straightforward terms, he is a man with nowhere to go; he has become identified with the hopelessness of sin, with human failure and frustration.

3 · The Human Pilgrimage – *Purgatorial Fire*

Our human life is inevitably a journey from the past into the future, and that can bring us pains which we should like to be able to escape. But to escape from that necessary condition of life is to escape from life itself; it is to attempt to be masters of our own destiny instead of allowing ourselves to be God's creatures. The end result of that is dead self-absorption, which is the substance of the ancient image of hell. Cold pride, the root of all sins, is fundamentally that decision to seize for ourselves and at our own choice those blessings which God desires to give us, for which we must be ready to wait and into the enjoyment of which we must be ready to grow.

The opposite of pride is of course humility; and humility, unlike pride, is characterized by hope. Against the self-absorbed, static satisfaction of pride, humility brings with it a for ever forward-looking yearning for a state which is not yet as it should be. Hopeful humility insists that where we are now is no resting place but only the beginning of a journey to some as yet unseen destination, a journey whose way is Jesus and whose goal is God. We can consider the nature of this journey of hope and humility by means of a fairy story, the particularly moving tale told by Hans Christian Andersen under the title, 'The Wild Swans'.

At the beginning of this story, eleven princes have been turned into swans by the magic of their wicked stepmother, and only their beautiful and innocent sister, the princess Elise, is left. At first, she has no knowledge of their altered form, and she searches for them high and low with no success. Then one day she sees eleven swans come down from the sky at sunset, and for the hours of darkness only they are returned to human shape. In joy she greets them, and hope is renewed within her as she learns that perhaps she can break the spell and release her brothers to their proper form for ever. But first she must travel with them into exile, far from her own native land. There she must weave for each of them a shirt, made out of flax which she herself has spun from stinging nettles; these nettles she must gather with her own hands at dead of night from the churchyards, among the graves. And for all the time it takes her to complete the task, she must not speak a single word or her brothers will be lost for ever.

Out of her great love for them, Elise flies off with her brothers into exile and begins her task, though the nettles burn her hands with fiery pain. One day, the king of that country meets her, and because she is the loveliest girl he has ever seen he takes her to his palace and makes her his wife. Now her task is harder still, for all around conspire to give her every luxury and cannot understand why she weeps if she is kept from her humble task of weaving flaxen shirts.

Elise has finished seven of the shirts, when the flax runs out. She must creep out again in secret to the graveyards, and there pick nettles, tread them with her bare feet into fibres and spin them into flax. But while she is among the graves, she is seen by the Archbishop of that place, who because of her silence already suspects her of being a witch. He denounces her to the king and to the people, and she is condemned to be burned at the stake for sorcery. She cannot protest her innocence, and now the burning pain in her hands and feet is matched by the pain in her heart because her husband (whom she has grown to love) has not trusted her, along with the terrible fear that she will be prevented from finishing the work to save her brothers. Still she continues to weave the shirts, in her prison cell and even on her last day, in the very cart which carries her to execution. Then at last, when she is at the stake itself, the swans, her brothers, fly to meet her; she throws the completed shirts over them and they are restored – all but the youngest, whose shirt Elise has not been able to complete and so he is left for ever with one swan's wing in place of a human arm.

Endurance beyond hope; at every turn a new danger to be met, a new pain to be suffered, a new humility to be learned. The innocent hope of Elise's childhood first dashed to the ground when her brothers disappear. The joyful hope with which she meets them again in their enchantment, turned into a never-ending agony. The high and courageous spirit with which she goes with them into exile, giving place to a fearful ignorance as to whether anything will avail at the end. Her trust in the king her husband as her loving protector, converted into deep sadness when he cannot or will not save her from the stake. It has been said that faith and hope and love are no virtues at all unless they believe and hope and love where it is impossible; to hope beyond possibility of hope, that is the hope of Elise.

This theme of hope enduring beyond hope, becoming purified as every visible hope is stripped away, is deeply embedded both in our experience and in the literature of our civilization, often in the shape of a never-ending journey to an ever-receding goal. Perhaps the most famous, as well as the most romantic, in European literature is the ancient story of the Quest of the Holy Grail, that sacred object of searching which continually hides itself from those who are not ready to see it, and whose full enjoyment comes only at the end of all our searching, with death itself. But the Scriptures too are shot through with the very same theme.

Consider the many wanderings of God's people, from Abraham's call to leave his native country for a land which God promises to give his descendants, through the many journeys of the patriarchs culminating in the departure of Jacob and all his family out of that Promised Land to dwell far away in Egypt. There they come to enjoy wealth and blessings at first, but slavery later. So they leave Egypt under Moses, heading back to the land once promised to their ancestors and now held out to them again. They reach its borders, only to find themselves unworthy of entering their promised land and turned away. Then forty years of wandering in the desert, at the end of which (with all but a handful of those who had originally departed from Egypt now dead) at last they begin to enter the hoped-for 'land of milk and honey'. But there they swiftly find themselves under the yoke of the Philistines, the native rulers of the land. New hope dawns with Saul, their first king, but he quickly degenerates into corruption. Then come the rise of David and the establishing of a secure capital at Jerusalem, and all the glory of Solomon and his Temple, only to be followed on Solomon's death by the tragedy of irreparable division into two rival kingdoms. There follows a long and sorry tale of rebellion against God and renewal, repeated rebellion and finally exile of both these kingdoms in turn and the destruction of Jerusalem. In exile, hope is renewed for a return from Babylon and rebuilding of the Temple, with further disillusionment at the way things actually turn out and the troubles and opposition which the returning exiles meet. Then finally, yet more captivities, this time on their own soil first under Greek then under Roman domination.

It is as though at every turn, whenever God's people

think they have arrived at last, whenever they think they can settle down and enjoy the fruit of their hopes, God says to them, 'Oh no, not yet; your journey is not over yet.' But still their hope persists, sometimes no more than a faint seed guarded by a tiny prophetic remnant. But fragile or not, the hopefulness is there, a trust in God's promises which is driven in the end to such ignorance about its object that it can at last be expressed only in visionary terms, a hope stretching beyond history itself, a hope for something – who knows what – something yet to be given beyond the final ending of all our history's hopes and fears.

This story of Israel reflects our continuing historical and personal experience, too. The earthly paradise is as far off now as ever it was, and still we must set our pilgrim faces towards it. Each new goal in life attained, each new sin overcome, each social good achieved, each new depth of relationship plumbed, brings with it a further horizon to which we must look, calling us still to move on and not fall into the temptation to become fixed at one stage in our story. The more we really achieve, the more precarious becomes our position, the more dangerous the threats which confront us. It has been said that one of the major reasons for the difficulties of marriage in our society now is that such high expectations are held regarding it today. The marriages which are in greatest danger of breaking up are also often those whose potential is the greatest, those where real communication and sharing has begun, where each partner is open and vulnerable to be given great joy or great, and even unendurable, pain by the other. On the wider historical plane, we all know how our age, which has seen such vast achievements and such strides forward in so many ways, lives also on the brink of disasters on a scale never even thinkable before. Sometimes, the price of pilgrimage seems too high; would it not be better to turn back, to 'go back to nature' as some wish to do, to revert to the so-called 'simple life' without the advantages, but also without the dangers and complexities, of modern civilization? It is sometimes still possible (despite the relatively easy option of divorce as an alternative in our day) to find a married couple who have gone adventurously to the brink of destruction in their marriage, and then pulled back into safety, into observing perhaps for their children's sake the social conventions, back into lifeless, non-communicating respectability.

Perhaps in some instances that may be necessary, the only way of coping with the situation. But in more general terms, and in the end, there can be no such turning back. 'Once the hand is laid on the plough,' says Jesus, 'no one who looks back is fit for the kingdom of God' (Luke 9.62). Once we have recognized the inadequacy of our present condition, the longing thus created in us will never again let us be content with it. The path of submission to God is a very dangerous path to take; the further we go, the greater is our need, the more tightly we are wound in God's clutches, the more certainly we find that to desert God brings disaster to our moral and personal life.

We return again to Dante's *Divine Comedy*, whose first part concerned hell, the symbol of all the self-absorbed deadliness of sin. The second part of Dante's poem is called 'Purgatory'. This is a medieval image for our human pilgrimage. The Church of England does not encourage us to believe in purgatory as a state beyond death; but it is a symbol which is certainly true to the reality of our journey here on earth. For it can be very painful to allow ourselves to move on from the past and not to cling to it, to give up old memories, relationships and achievements, to acknowledge old failures as done and finished with, no longer open to correction. Yet this painful purging of attachment to the past is absolutely necessary if we are to grow, to mature, to be alive. It can be very painful to allow our future to be guided by events and circumstances and other people, not to seek control over an uncertain future but to accept it at God's hand. Yet this painful purging of attachment to our own vision of the future is absolutely necessary if we are to be truly at the service of God and go by the way which God desires for us.

In the vision of Dante's poem, purgatory is an exactly inverted replica of hell. Hell is a vast, funnel-shaped pit digging into the very centre of the earth, and at its lowest point is Satan, the source of all its evil. Purgatory is an equally vast, cone-shaped mountain on the opposite side of the world from the mouth of hell, and at its highest point it touches heaven, the source of all its hope. For purgatory, the human pilgrimage, is essentially a state of hope. On the sides of the mountain, toiling up the spiral path which winds around it towards the summit, Dante finds exactly the same range of sinners as he had found in hell. One thing only distinguishes them: the sinners on Mount Purgatory have repented. They have turned their faces away from their sinfulness towards God; they have made the crucial decision that God's will and not their own shall govern their lives. Now on the mountain of pilgrimage they are going through the process of allowing God gradually to strip away every attachment so that they may give themselves fully and wholeheartedly to that divine will which they have in principle already accepted once for all. They live in hope of God; but in that hope, every created hope is stripped away.

To be human is to be on pilgrimage, to change over time; there is no such thing as a static, unchanging, once for all achieved humanity. For to be human is to be involved with others, to be involved in personal relationships; and one thing above all that is distinctive about personal relationships is that they take time to begin, time to develop, to deepen, to enjoy, and sometimes to decay.

There is a class of personal relationship, to which I have already referred, of which this is above all true; and that is marriage. There is a sense in which it might be better to speak of a marriage not as a single relationship at all, but a series of relationships. The way in which my wife and I relate to each other now, with our only daughter at university, my wife working half time and me full time, is different from the way we related when our daughter was at school and we both worked full time; different from the way we related before our daughter went to school, when I was a parish priest and my wife at home all day; different from our relationship before our daughter was born, when we wanted and later were expecting a child; different again from the earliest years, when I was a student on a grant, my wife the breadwinner, and a baby was the last thing we desired. Nor of course has it all ended now; when our daughter has set up a home of her own, when we have retired, when one of us has died, all these will be times for our relating to be learned afresh, new changes in the form of our marriage.

Yet it is after all the same marriage at every stage, and not a succession of different marriages. The vows which we made to each other at the beginning are still the vows by which we must live. We are not engaged in making new commitments to each other, but in finding deeper meaning in the one commitment which we then made once for all.

The same is true of our pilgrimage with God. From day to day, from one place to another, its form is very different, sometimes almost unrecognizably so; and yet all that is happening is that we are discovering again and again and again, more and more deeply, what it means to make that one act of hope and humility and penitence in which we recognize our need of God. With more and more certainty, each time life holds out to us its hopes and we discover either that they cannot be achieved or else that they are not what we really wanted after all, we, like God's ancient people, have all particular and concrete hopes stripped away. More and more we learn to submit to that discipline which once and for all has seized upon us – the discipline of resting content with absolutely no state of affairs in our history at all, no achievements at all; the discipline of ever greater patience, the discipline by which we learn not to leap at any proferred goal as if it were the end and completion of our journey. Whether it may be getting married, or having children, getting a new job, moving house, succeeding in a particularly important project, reaching retirement, or whatever goal it is, we learn again and again that each end is only a new beginning, only a place for renewed turning back to God, and the ever receding goal of our pilgrimage has still not yet arrived.

4 · THE CRUCIFIED – *PURGATION*

IT IS ON the cross that Jesus completely shares all that is most intolerable and hopeless in our condition; and it is on the cross that he completes his lifelong pilgrimage, the process by which he does penance for human sin. Here he is stripped of every attachment, every bond of friendship, every source of satisfaction. Here he learns by bitter experience what it is to be human, caught midway between the beasts and the angels, between the past and the present, searching for hope as hope after hope is taken away.

We are told very little of the inner workings of Jesus' mind; just the occasional hint of deep sorrow. For the rest we have to draw our conclusions from the fact of his common humanity with ourselves, or else remain in ignorance. But even without such knowledge, we can say something from the events themselves. What can we say of the process of his failure – the shape of his enduring of it – and what it does to this man who goes through it?

His friends, the inner company chosen to share and carry on his work, have been blind to the last and now have run away; there is one source of hope removed. Peter, to be sure, has regained courage and followed him to the high priest's house; but we know what has happened to Peter there. According to Luke, at the cock-crow Jesus turns and looks at Peter, hoping against hope, perhaps, not to see written on Peter's face the shame and defeat he has known from the first will be there. On Peter, the effect of the meeting is devastating: 'He went outside and wept bitterly' (Luke 22.62). But what does it do to Jesus?

Perhaps some hope remains that at the last the truth will be heard; or at least that imperial justice will recognize and reject the malice which accuses him. But no. His open claim before the priests to be Messiah becomes the occasion of taunting and jeering, as they indulge in a kind of experimental disproof of it: 'If you're the Son of God, tell us who hit you! But you can't!' (cf. Matt. 26.67–8). The very best that his innocence is ever in danger of earning him from Pilate is to be 'let off with a flogging' (Luke 23.16). Not that even this hope survives for long. Another possibility gone.

Then there is the matter of Judas. Jesus is compelled to see his hope for this man, the hope which led him to call the man as an apostle, come to nothing. He has indeed 'called a sinner', and it is proving to be to his own destruction and to that sinner's damnation. In how many other cases does he wonder if it may not be the same? Another hope shattered.

What then of his hope in God? What does he expect from his long prayer in Gethsemane? To be freed from the necessity of having to die? To be granted at least a simple death, with no added torments on the way? To have the strength to die a silent, noble, martyr's death? But every possible favourable answer to his prayer is stripped away, until he is left with nothing but the prayer itself, nothing but the bare process of humiliation. That prayer in the garden, 'My Father, if it is possible, let this cup pass me by. Nevertheless, let it be as you, not I, would have it' (Matt. 26.39), gives place to his later prayer, 'My God, my God, why have you forsaken me?' (Matt. 27.46). Still to the end he is searching, still wrestling with his pain, still the pain is painful for him. This is no noble, silent death in calm heroism unaffected by what they are doing to him. This man is affected by it, he is truly hurt by the pain; he falls, he thirsts, he cries aloud in dereliction. He is being subjected to a humiliating process, a dehumanizing process; he is not insulating himself from it, but letting it happen to him.

Perhaps here may be found a key to the mystery of his silence. Why is he silent before his accusers? 'Like a lamb led to the slaughter-house, like a sheep dumb in front of its shearers' (Acts 8.32, quoting Isaiah 53.7); yes, but sheep have no choice in the matter; people make up their minds whether to speak or stay silent. So why is he silent?

Is it perhaps that he, too, really has no choice – no moral choice? Is there a real sense in which the accusations brought against him are in fact true? He has indeed been threatening the fabric of their society and religion, he is indeed a menace to social and political stability. No matter that he believed he had good cause and authority for his actions; no matter that his accusers may in the last resort be condemning themselves by bringing these charges at all and not rather acknowledging his claims. To the charges as listed there is only one answer he can give, and that is 'Guilty'. By framing the case against him as they have, by concentrating on just those things which he cannot truthfully deny, even by the sheer act of putting him up before the representative of an imperial authority whose absolute claims to power are bound to be challenged by his gospel, they have effectively robbed him of the right to defend himself. They have added one more ingredient to the process by which they rob him of humanity, taken one more hope away from him.

I am reminded, when thinking of the silence of Jesus, of the silence of Thomas More before his accusers as portrayed in the play *A Man for all Seasons*. More has been accused of a crime of which he is. indeed morally guilty (in his case, of denying that the King of England could set himself up as Head of the Church). His real defence is that it ought not to be a crime at all, and in trying him on such a charge his accusers are displaying their own degradation. So he is silent in his own defence; he will not deny what he holds to be the truth, but he will not incriminate himself by saying openly the words which have been declared by the King and Parliament to be treasonable. More's silence is his last hope for survival. Is Jesus' silence then like that, the only stand he can make for truth and integrity without inevitably forfeiting his life? If so, that hope too is dashed away. Not only is it no defence, it is used by the soldiers as an excuse for subjecting him to yet more torment, yet more mockery and brutalization just to see (we can suppose) how much he is really prepared to take.

So in the end he is silent without any hope of good from it at all, silently suffering because that is all that is left for him to do. He has become identified with the purging suffering of our human pilgrimage.

5 · The Human Pilgrimage – *Ever-Present Hope*

In folktale and romance, a very popular theme is that of the great quest whose object is finally found at the wanderer's own door. Lazy Jack goes off in search of the pot of gold, and after many years comes home to find it hidden in his own back yard. Two idle brothers are left a treasure of gold which they are told is hidden somewhere in the orchard, and after many years' hard work, digging between all the trees to find it, they discover that their treasure is the golden fruit on the trees which their labour has unknowingly cultivated. The pilgrim searches high and low, and finally returns to find that what he was looking for was by his side all along, unnoticed because so near at hand.

This can result in deep and bitter tragedy, when the wanderer comes so late to realization of the truth that the time has passed to benefit from it. It is this that makes Shakespeare's *King Lear* so frightening a reminder of the tragic potential of all our lives. At the beginning of the play, Lear has decided to divide his kingdom among his daughters; but first, he tests their worthiness by asking them to say how much they love him. His older daughters protest their love in extravagant words, which later prove completely insincere. But when the love which Lear is seeking is offered to him by his youngest daughter Cordelia, he cannot recognize it. Her words are too homely, too ordinary, too truthful as compared with her sisters' high-flown promises. The whole ensuing play is a presentation of his ever more frenzied search for love after he has banished the only one who could have given it to him, and then his growing inability to accept love when it is offered again.

Finally, Lear does come to his senses, he sees and accepts in Cordelia's down to earth, realistic care that love which he has been desiring all along, but by then, a train of events has already been set in motion that leads inexorably to her death while he stands helpless to prevent it. Such a situation cries out for a saviour, for someone who can undo the dreadful knot tied by past evil so that hard-won wisdom and humble insight can come to something. But the play ends as tragedy, for no saviour is given.

The truth which this kind of tragedy tells us in its sombre way is simple, direct, very obvious, and extremely costly in the accepting of it: if we cannot find heaven, the Holy Grail, true love, the pot of gold, happiness, here and now in the ordinary daily affairs of life, we shall never find it at all. And there is really not the contradiction which at first sight might appear between this truth and the equal truth that here and now we have not reached our goal, but must always journey hopefully on endless pilgrimage. It is not Lear's frenzied searching for love and his failure to find it in the places he expected that is tragic; on the contrary, his repeated rejection by those who had claimed to love him above all things, his repeated disillusion in those hopes, is precisely what finally leaves him helpless, alone, able to accept the love of Cordelia because there is nothing else left for him to do. In the same way, a hope which has been purged of every concrete object whatsoever, a hope that has learned to face our present condition with utter realism, a hope that has suffered every possible disillusionment and remains blindly looking forward, not knowing what it has to hope for, such a hope alone is able to release us to live fully in the present moment, taking each moment's actual challenge as it comes.

Any concrete hope at all, which looks to a particular future goal, will tend inevitably to fix our hearts upon that goal, and so prevent us from noticing the glories and the opportunities of the world confronting us now. But absolute hope, hope stripped naked of any actual expectation, has the very opposite effect. It enables us to see every present situation, whatever it may be, as full of hope. That is why Jesus, who time and again proclaims the hope of God's coming Kingdom, can also say 'Do not worry about tomorrow; tomorrow will take care of itself' (Matt. 6.34). Absolute hope, the blind expectancy that God's Kingdom will come in utter ignorance of the shape which that Kingdom will take, enables us to welcome and respond to every present moment as the situation in which that Kingdom can become real.

So our Christian hope does not deny the reality of this world's concerns; very far from it. The 'Kingdom of heaven' (which is little more than the phrase which we use for want of any other to label the unknown object of our hope) is itself the very meaning of all our worldly affairs. When we have found the true significance of the world of everyday work, of politics and social action, of science and engineering, of washing-up and clearing breakfast, of mowing the lawn and going shopping, of birthday parties and watching children grow, even of famine and sickness and violence, when we have found the real meaning of that world, then we have found heaven.

We do not find God by roaming far away from ordinary life into some lofty realm of pure religion; we do not achieve social harmony by fixing our eyes on some ideal world which bears no relation to our situation here and now. Yet, at the same time, we do not find the true meaning of our world by clinging to such meaning as we have already found, or seizing upon new meanings and new goals, as those who built a tower at Babel tried to cling and Adam tried to seize the forbidden fruit. The process of recognition of this world's true meaning is more secret than that, more subtle, taking us more by surprise.

In Northamptonshire there is a most unusual place of pilgrimage. It is a tiny hamlet, or less than a hamlet, just a farm and a church, called Little Gidding. There in the seventeenth century a Christian community lived a life of discipline and charity, led by a Cambridge don named Nicholas Ferrar, who gave up his fellowship to live in simple holiness. Among the many people who have been deeply impressed by that place in our day was the poet T. S. Eliot, who found in Little Gidding the inspiration for the last of his sequence of poems, *Four Quartets*:

If you came at night like a broken king,
If you came by day not knowing what you came for,
It would be the same, when you leave the rough road
And turn behind the pig-sty to the dull façade
And the tombstone. And what you thought you came for
Is only a shell, a husk of meaning
From which the purpose breaks only when it is fulfilled
If at all.

T. S. Eliot
Little Gidding, I lines 26–33

For that particular place of pilgrimage is (or was, when I was last there) just like that, unexpected even when you arrive. No great signs announcing that you are drawing near to a holy place, no directions for coaches and cars to park; only a rough farm road with a muddy ending, a gate into a field, and a little chapel round the corner, hidden at first from view. It comes quite by surprise, and it is quite unassuming when it comes. Yet in all its unassuming ordinariness, it imposes its own lowliness on the visitor, breaking down every preconception and insisting that it is just itself:

> If you came this way,
> Taking any route, starting from anywhere,
> At any time or at any season,
> It would always be the same: you would have to put off
> Sense and notion. You are not here to verify,
> Instruct yourself, or inform curiosity
> Or carry report. You are here to kneel
> Where prayer has been valid.

T. S. Eliot
Little Gidding I lines 39–46

Unpremeditated, unpretentious, unplanned simplicity. How often is that our experience of real happiness? It comes when least expected, not planned for but stealing up on us unawares, as the almost accidental by-product of doing a job with someone whom you love, being engrossed in some absorbing interest, being lost in the magic of a place. Sometimes we do not even notice it until after the moment has passed, and only then do we look back on it as a moment of simple joy. We have to learn to be in heaven by accident.

Because the world of every day, in which we are to find heaven given to us, is always changing, never still, heaven always remains to be discovered afresh. As the great medieval English teacher of prayer, Mother Julian of Norwich, has it, 'We are for ever being born of Christ our Saviour, and shall never be delivered!'

(*Revelations of Divine Love*, 57). The never-ending search is itself also the always renewed offer of heaven. The ever-receding goal is our guarantee that the offer will never cease to be made to us, that we never in any situation or at any time can cease to hope; for always there is more to come.

In a world which exists in time, we are bound to share in a certain restlessness, if we allow ourselves to belong to that world at all without evading it in complacency or despair. But that very restlessness, to all appearances merely the result of our existing as changing, growing beings in time, that very hope for change is the created aspect of the divine creativity which we call 'heaven'. For it is ultimately God who is unceasingly restless, always yearning to give us richer and richer gifts of grace, to draw us on to greater and greater glory. Our being in time, our way of pilgrimage, even that sense of homelessness, that sense of the loss of our traditions, which has been identified as one of the marks and pains of our modern society, all is but a reflection of God's absolute and unending creativity. When we know that, then we become able to enjoy that creative restlessness here and now, within the limitations of our present condition, in the ordinary tasks of our daily calling. God's own creativity is the real meaning, the true sense and significance, of our worldly and practical endeavours.

The mistake and fault of humanity as represented by Adam in the myth of Eden is that, feeling the creative restlessness within ourselves, we look only to the plain object of our yearning in the present, the forbidden fruit, and take it; so we are sunk in the world as it is. Adam – which means all of us – has to unlearn that fatal mistake, so as to grow able to recognize the divine meaning of our restlessness. 'Anyone who has seen me,' Jesus says to his disciples, 'has seen the Father' (John

14.9). The human life is in itself the presence and glory of God.

We return again to *The Divine Comedy.* After tracing the descent into self-absorbed pride in hell, and passing from there to the mountain of purifying pilgrimage in purgatory, in the third part of the poem Dante is given a vision of heaven. And just as in purgatory he had found penitent sinners who had committed the same sins whose penalty he had observed in unrepentant hell, so too in heaven the same sins are found again, but now redeemed and made the substance of glory. The saints in heaven are allotted ranks according to their lives on earth, so that the character of those lives is not simply wiped out as though they had never been. The substance of heaven is nothing more or less than our experience here on earth and what by God's grace we have made of it. But whereas our experience on earth is characterized by restlessness, each saint in heaven is utterly content with the rank assigned to him or her; for each one knows that it is just the right place, and no other would be fitting. All the saints in heaven know this because their gaze is directed unceasingly to God, in whose love the many different kinds of human strengths and weaknesses all fall into place.

The difference between heaven and hell is not in the moral character of those who are in either state, not in what they have said or done in itself, but solely in this: any action, any character, however good, which looks in upon itself alone is the stuff of hell; but the same action, the same character, however bad, if only we are willing to look beyond its outward face to see its place in God's creative love, can also be the stuff of heaven; and our existence here on earth is always the purging, purifying pilgrimage from the first of these attitudes towards the second.

In Dante's final vision of the saints in heaven, they all

in their ordered ranks form the petals of an enormous rose, whose centre is God; they are all at the same time bright, fiery points of light. In medieval literature, the rose was the symbol of earthly love, and so it stands for this life with all its everyday concerns. In Dante's vision, this life and every love within this life have been transformed and purified by the purging fire so that they reveal their true, inner meaning, and shine with the light of God.

We shall not cease from exploration
And the end of all our exploring
Will be to arrive where we started
And know the place for the first time.
Through the unknown, remembered gate
When the last of earth left to discover
Is that which was the beginning;
At the source of the longest river
The voice of the hidden waterfall
And the children in the apple-tree
Not known, because not looked for
But heard, half-heard, in the stillness
Between two waves of the sea.
Quick now, here, now, always –
A condition of complete simplicity
(Costing not less than everything)
And all shall be well and
All manner of thing shall be well
When the tongues of flame are in-folded
Into the crowned knot of fire
And the fire and the rose are one.

T. S. Eliot
Little Gidding V, lines 25–45

It has been suggested that we are all of us – even if we do not know it – involved in a love affair with God. Like lovers trying to attract the attention of their beloved, we posture before God, we get up to all kinds of tricks of religion and morality to try to show ourselves off before God. Sometimes – too, too often – we are tricked by our own posturing, we take it all so seriously, we think that it finally matters what we do; but when we are like that, then whether what we do is bad or good we are stuck in sin, our noses pressed hard against our own reflections and unable to see any further. To come to realize the deadliness of this is at once the first act of penitence and the never-ending painful process of purgation. But to be given the realization of it, to know our foolishness as the rather comical expression of our stumbling love, and to know it as accepted in all its stumbling foolishness by the infinite love of God, that itself is heaven.

O world invisible, we view thee,
O world intangible, we touch thee,
O world unknowable, we know thee,
Inapprehensible, we clutch thee!

Does the fish soar to find the ocean,
The eagle plunge to find the air –
That we ask of the stars in motion
If they have rumour of thee there?

Not where the wheeling systems darken,
And our benumb'd conceiving soars! –
The drift of pinions, would we hearken,
Beats at our own clay-shuttered doors.

The angels keep their ancient places; –
Turn but a stone, and start a wing!
'Tis ye, 'tis your estrangèd faces,
That miss the many-splendour'd thing.

But (when so sad thou canst not sadder)
Cry – and upon thy so sore loss
Shall shine the traffic of Jacob's ladder
Pitched betwixt Heaven and Charing Cross.

Yea, in the night, my Soul, my daughter,
Cry – clinging Heaven by the hems;
And lo, Christ walking on the water,
Not of Gennesareth, but Thames!

Francis Thompson
'In No Strange Land'

6 · The Crucified – *Victory*

The story of Calvary is a historical story of failure, the failure of goodness to be recognized, to be accepted and to win out. It is a true story of suffering, the systematic stripping away from a real man of everything that can be stripped away which enriches his humanity. And, it is claimed by the Christian tradition, it is also a story of victory and glory. But if that is true, then it is a victory won and a glory gained only in and through the failure and the suffering, and not despite them. We have no right to make jewelled crosses or to put up figures of Christ in majesty until we have learned to see that majesty in the real crucified one, the suffering, failed man of Calvary.

The glory of the cross is indeed paradoxical; it is the glory of the cross. It is the glory hinted at by the observation that, failure as this man is, it may be better to have failed at trying what he has tried than to have succeeded in anything else in the world. It is the glory suggested by the question, 'When he suffers at his tormentors' hands, and they in concert seek to dehumanize him by his suffering, who is really being dehumanized and who is finding truly human dignity?'

It is the glory proclaimed in that wonderfully ambiguous final cry in John's Gospel, 'It is finished' (John 19.30). He has come to the end of the road; but he has indeed come right to the end, without pulling back. And there is the glory of it.

What does that mean, 'He has come right to the end of the road, without pulling back'? It means that he has committed himself so totally to the Kingdom of God's love that he will not act in any way at all which compromises the claims of that Kingdom, even when this means that no action whatever remains open to him and he can only suffer at the mercy of events and of the enemies of love. It means that he has followed the path of his proclamation so far that he cannot now see any way in which that proclamation can be fulfilled; and yet he continues to proclaim it. Further than that: he has reached the point where any action taken by him to avoid his own destruction will falsify, contradict and fatally compromise the truth of his message; for he cannot act now without compromising his love, the love which he has taught must extend even to his enemies. Yet if he is destroyed his message will surely perish with him, for no-one at all is left who can be trusted to carry it on. He has reached the point beyond all hope, where all that he can do is to go on. The victory, the glory, lies just in this, that even at that point he does go on.

What does he go on doing? The answer is simple, straightforward and down-to-earth. He goes on submitting his whole being utterly to the Father; he goes on loving those before him who need his love. To the first, we have unanimous testimony from all four evangelists; to the second, we have the witness (in different ways) of Luke and of John.

I suppose we are all likely to know the self-absorbing effect which pain can have upon us. We can, perhaps, muster up enough goodwill not to be a burden to others when we are sick, or in any kind of trouble; but to pay real attention to others' troubles from the centre of our own, that takes holiness of a different order. Yet this is what Jesus does, from the cross itself. Here you might have thought he would be immune from the crowding pressures of those who need his ministrations. But no. There are enemies to forgive, there is his mother to provide for, there is a fellow-convict on the next cross who cries out for hope. In every case, he responds with love. But behind all this is the more fundamental turning beyond himself: his unceasing gaze towards God. In the same two Gospels which give us these human scenes, we hear of this in a pretty straightforward way. Luke's final, trusting cry, 'Father, into your hands I commit my spirit' (Luke 23.46), and in John the whole shape and tone of the entire story tell of the same unwavering devotion to the Father's will. But even that cry which is the only intelligible word from the cross in Mark and Matthew, even that dreadful 'My God, my God, why have you forsaken me?' (Mark 15.34; Matt. 27.46), conveys the same message; for even that is still a prayer. Even in his dereliction, at the bottom of the pit of failure and the most abject nakedness of all hope, it is God to whom he turns, God's way and will that he is still trying to fathom. There is his victory. There is what makes him the most human figure in that whole scene, despite every outward effect of dehumanization. His total dependence on the Father even when the Father can no longer be found, and his persistent care for his brethren even when they betray him, desert him, revile him and crucify him.

'Even when they betray him.' Even towards Judas the end of the story of Jesus is that he loves him. He loves him enough to permit him to damn himself, if that is what he is intent on doing; just as God still loves each of us enough to let us make our evil choices, loves us enough never to try to force love out of us by compulsion. The dreadful risk which Jesus takes with Judas – a risk which in his case was (as far as we can tell) a failure – is the risk love always takes if it is really love and not some selfish substitute; and so the very taking of it is love's triumph. Love is still love, no matter what love's enemies can do.

Yet still we have not reached the height and depth of that love of Jesus. When the Israelites were wandering in the desert, they complained against God time and time again. On one occasion, so the story runs, they were punished by a plague of fiery snakes. Moses prayed for their deliverance, and in answer God told him to make a bronze image of a snake; and whoever was bitten by one of the snakes and looked at that image would be healed of the poison of the bite. That was the snake which Moses lifted up in the desert (Num. 21.4–9).

The Israelites were healed by looking at the image of the punishment sent for their sin, by having their attention directed to their fault and its reward. And this is the meaning of the cross of Jesus. It is judgement on our fallenness, the evidence of our sin. In being judged by the cross, in hearing and receiving the truth which it proclaims about us, we are saved.

This is the divine twist in the serpent's tail, which enables us to call this Friday 'Good'. Evil is made to work its own destruction, through the facing of the truth. The greater the evil, the more clearly its character stands out; in the killing of Jesus it is apparent in its nakedness for all to see. So we are rescued from its grip. When we accept the cross of Jesus as the centre of our world, we accept our fallenness, our inability to make good of ourselves; we are compelled to set our hope in God alone. But that hope is exactly the hope which nothing can destroy, and which everything can feed. When we know that nothing less than God can give us hope, then nothing which is less than God can turn us aside from our hope in God, and everything can be the place where hope is found.

So even in the judgement on our sin which the cross unwaveringly makes, the love of God is at work. That love is the love which Jesus shows to the very end, the love to which he gives his life, the love from which he draws his whole existence. That love overcomes and turns to love's advantage everything which sets itself against it. Such love as that can never be destroyed.

7 · INTERLUDE – *REFLECTIONS OF A BYSTANDER*

WE WENT OUTSIDE the city today to watch an execution. The usual thing, a disgusting spectacle – so appalling our eyes were somehow drawn to it despite our loathing. A sight of blood and pain, three bodies tortured to death to prove the might of Rome. Less than human they seemed, tattered remnants of flesh and blood set up by the roadside for a dreadful warning.

Less than human – and yet how totally human they were. United on their crosses in their pain, their shame, and in the one thing that will unite us all – death. We tried not to stare, embarrassed at the naked suffering before us, fearful of the truth of our humanity their dying brought home to us. Some of us sought to cast out the demon of our own fear by throwing it onto them, with angry, frightened taunts and jeers. Loading our bitterness, our fear, our frustration, our pain onto those who couldn't cast it back at us; onto them, as they hung in helpless torment as if just made to be victims for our mockery.

And especially onto him. The one in the centre, the one we had taken for a prophet, the one we had mistaken for a holy man, the one we had even been fools enough to think might be the long-awaited Son of God. What business had the Son of God to be helpless? What right had a prophet to let them – let us – do that to him? Where was his God now, the God in whom he claimed to trust, the God he knew as 'Father', the God he said was our God too? Where was this loving God at his Messiah's hour of need?

Where was God in *our* time of need? Where was God in the wars which killed our sons and daughters, where was God at the failure of our hopes and dreams, where was God in our fears and in our pain? When we cried out to God, and our prayers were not answered? When we looked for a miracle, and no miracle was given? Where was God then? When our children were born with terrible deformities, when our aged parents descended into a sub-human state that sent a shiver of fear through us as we saw in them our own decay, when the growing menace of fearful disease held us back from human decency for fear the one we cared for might be a carrier – where was God then? Where was the God who made this world of helplessness and pain? Where was the God who called us out to be his people, the God who through the centuries has demanded our faithful obedience and our unswerving loyalty? Where was God's loyal faithfulness to us, in the hour of our pain?

So we cast our fury at him, this man who claimed to speak for God. We found in him a way to get our own back for all the hurts we had suffered at God's hands. The hands which claimed to do the work of God we saw fixed by nails to a cross, and we were glad. The face which we had thought might show us the truth of God we saw dripping with blood from a crown of thorns, and we rejoiced. At last we had a worthy outlet for our frustrated anger; he identified himself with God and with God's purposes – then let him take God's punishment, the reward for a God who had created us, created a universe, and failed to make it free of pain. 'His blood be on us, and on our children.' For our blood was on God, and on God's Son.

Our blood on him. The blood of our suffering and of

our grief, running down his face, his arms, his side. He hung there, battered by our taunts, but strangely he was not broken. No answering hatred escaped his lips, no bitterness directed against us or against the God who had forsaken him. Some even said they heard a prayer for our forgiveness emerge between the gasps of his agony. Sheer folly – or something else, something far beyond all our imagining? Some said he spoke to the tortured body beside him on the other cross, offering comfort from out of the depths of his own pain, and quiet assurance of hope in the centre of that place of hopelessness. Some heard a calm assurance of his own at the very end, as he gave his life to God; others heard only a continued struggling with the mystery of God in his isolation and agony, refusing to turn away from God even when God seemed to have deserted him. But on some of us there slowly dawned a kind of awe, as we came to see that here indeed – in him above all others at that scene – was true humanity, alive, victorious amidst all that was conspiring to destroy it. Less than human? No; supremely human, with a real humanity which put ours to shame.

And strangely, standing there, we found within ourselves a kind of peace. Our anger all was spent, our fury had burst out and done its worst; and still the face which met the onslaught of our pain was the face of unconquered love. Then at last, a new wonder struck our hearts; was this the answer to all our questioning, was this after all the place where God was in our pain? Was this bleeding face of human helplessness, this tortured face of love, in truth, the face of God?

PART TWO

Easter Day

8 · The Many-Sided Victory

In nomine Patris et Filii et Spiritus Sancti. In the resurrection of Jesus, we enter the world of a strange tongue. *Alleluia. Hosanna. Kyrie eleison.* How many of the words and phrases and titles we use in Christian worship, how many of the words which occur in the Christian story, come to us from the mysterious recesses of an alien age in a foreign language. *Abba,* Father; *Eli, Eli, lama sabachthani; Alpha* and *Omega; Adonai; Maranatha; Rabboni; Christe eleison;* and even, *Amen.* And on Easter Day of all days we touch on the deep secret which is at the heart of all things; the paltry futility of all our shallow rationalizing is exposed.

What do we think we celebrate on Easter Sunday at the crack of dawn? What do we suppose the resurrection of Jesus to be? Some people will tell you that it is a matter of our meeting the risen Lord here and now, our finding him alive in our own experience. And so it is. But that cannot be all that it is. For we have learned to understand our experience in this way, because we have inherited the Christian culture. If we had been born in another age, another society, another culture, we should have learned to see in some other way those experiences of renewal, of new strength, of the divine presence, of joy, which we have learned to associate with the name of Jesus. So that account of his resurrection is not enough. *Kyrie eleison.*

Some people say that when we talk of the resurrection, we really mean the renewal of the lives of the apostles and those other first Christians, their reawakening to a conviction of the love and power of God after the disillusion of the death of Jesus. That is in itself, they say, a miraculous reawakening. And so it is. But that cannot be all that we mean by his resurrection. For the apostles came to life again not by some spontaneous rebirth of enthusiasm for no particular cause, but because they believed that something had happened independently of themselves. The apostles did not believe in their own resurgence of faith; they believed in something about God and about Jesus, something which they saw as justifying (and not merely causing) their new-found commitment. If we just believed in the renewal of the apostles, and this were all that we meant by the resurrection, we should in the very act be denying the basis which the apostles themselves gave for their renewal. So that account of his resurrection is not enough. *Christe eleison.*

Some people say that the place where Jesus lives is in the Church; in the real, living witness and action of Christians through the centuries. And so it is. But that cannot be all that it is. Simply think of the Church as it has actually been. Consider the crimes perpetrated in its name, the blind alleys, the worldliness, the unfaithfulness. Remember that the Church is nothing more than ourselves its members, and consider the degree of faithfulness to the way of Christ which we achieve. Recall how frequently we slip into forgetfulness, carelessness of the needs of others, and plain unthinking folly even at the very times of our highest spiritual exaltation. And then ask 'Is that all that I mean by the risen life of Christ? Is this Church – this us – really worth all the celebration of Easter Day?' The more realistically I try to look at the Church, the more I see how its only justification must lie outside itself, somewhere greater than its own weaknesses. So to identify the resurrection of Christ with the life and witness of the Church is another account that is not enough. *Kyrie eleison.*

Some people say that the body which died on Good Friday and was buried in Joseph's tomb actually came to life again. Only a really historical event could have had the shattering effect on people's lives which we know there to have been. The resurrection is not just a dream or wishful thinking or a way of talking about some subjective feelings which we have. If the resurrection of Jesus Christ is to be the foundation of our faith, then it must be real, true, an objective fact. And so it must. But that cannot be all that has to be said about it. For if you ask yourself what in fact it was that happened, I think you will find it exceedingly difficult – if not impossible – to think of it in any other way than as a dead person coming back to life again. Just as we are told that Jairus' daughter and Lazarus and the widow's son at Nain were brought back to life by Jesus, so Jesus himself came back to life. But that is precisely what Christians do not suppose the resurrection of Jesus to be! Whatever it was, it was not a return to more of this life but a progress to that which lies beyond this life; it is the triumphant move forwards into a completely new realm, not the resuscitation of dead relics. So that account of his resurrection is not enough. *Christe eleison.*

Some people say that the resurrection of Jesus is really a way of speaking about the true meaning of the whole of his life and death. We think about this man, we think about the pattern of his life and teaching, and the manner of his death, and it dawns on us that it is all true: his way of life was not a foolish delusion, his death was not a useless waste. On the contrary, this man's life and death tell us of the most profound of human and even divine realities. They speak to us of the way things really are with us, and between ourselves and God. It is this abiding truth of everything for which the natural life and death of Jesus stand that really constitutes his risen life. And so it does. But that cannot be all that there is to it. If we think that this account is enough, then I believe we have not yet reckoned sufficiently with the real horror and tragedy of his death, the real sense in which his teaching and example were a failure, the real futility of his natural life taken by itself. If we have only the meaning of his natural life and death to go to, we may have an example of grand heroism, but we have also a standing, unrelieved indictment of human weakness, folly and wickedness, and a lasting, tragic witness to the unrealistic romanticism of trying to live as Jesus lived. Whatever his resurrection is, it needs to be enough to alter that, to give to his life and death a meaning which of themselves they do not fully possess, to make all that for which he stood not merely a wonderful, wistful dream but actually true. An approach to the resurrection which sees in it only the way of perceiving the meaning already present in his life and death cannot begin to do that. So that account is not enough. *Kyrie eleison.*

So we might go on with other ideas about the kind of thing the resurrection could be; and we should find that not a single one of them would fit completely. For the resurrection of Jesus Christ is not a kind of thing at all, but something quite unique in human experience so far. There is no rational category in terms of which we can understand it, no description we can give which works entirely. We can be sure that we are speaking of something real, and not simply nothing at all, because we can see that there is some truth in all these incomplete accounts of it. If from our experience we can say that we believe in some of these things – in a continuing experience of Christ with us now, in the historical witness of the amazing new life given to the dispirited disciples, in the continuing of Christ's work through his living body, the Church, in the reality of the strange events connected with his body after death by crucifixion, in the abiding truth of everything for which he stood – if some of these really have meaning in our lives and experience, then we can say that we share the faith of the resurrection. But the more deeply we consider those approaches to it which mean the most to us, the more we shall discover that by themselves they are not enough; there are always more sides to it than we have yet discovered. The resurrection of Jesus Christ takes us into a world which breaks out of normal rules of understanding, a world where we leave the intelligible behind and must in the last resort speak a foreign tongue. That is itself the reason for our rejoicing in it! *Christus resurrexit! Alleluia!*

To put that slightly differently, the resurrection refuses to stand still and allow us to theorize about it; that is the way in which we know that we are here in touch with reality. The various theories together form a kind of wheel, rather like those modern versions of a Catherine wheel, in which several straightforward fireworks are bound together in a circle; each individual firework forms part of the circle's rim, and the fuse is connected in such a way that it ignites them all at once. As soon as they are lit, the whole construction begins to turn, until it becomes a moving wheel of fire. Traditional Catherine wheels were often the most disappointing kind of firework, because they tended to stick and then there was only a very boring single jet of flame moving round and round the spiral. These more sophisticated versions are in less danger of that, because the several jets all work at once from many directions all around the ring, and each is helping the others to spin the wheel around.

In just such a way do all the partial truths about the resurrection, each of which we can in some measure grasp, correct and complement each other, and create a living wheel of fire. If we focus our attention on one partial truth alone, and identify that single perspective with the meaning of the resurrection itself, our wheel will stick, or only fitfully revolve.

The pattern is the same whenever we are confronted by true reality, by the things of God. Nothing which we say can touch the mystery of God, and yet we cannot always remain silent. So we do the best we can with our words, using images, metaphors and analogies to express something of the mystery. By these partial approaches, we circle around. Though we never succeed in hitting the centre, the unutterable reality of the being of God, yet all our attempts together – so long as we continue moving and do not rely on one image alone – can take us by degrees and by a very roundabout route ever closer to that Mystery which we cannot reach by all our thinking and our speaking.

There is another kind of wheel of which many theologies of our day have spoken, and that is the wheel known sometimes as the hermeneutical circle, sometimes as the pastoral cycle. The basic image of a moving wheel is just the same, but the parts of its rim are not a series of theological theories but the stages in a whole programme of Christian discipleship. Because they are essentially stages in a changing process, this image can help us to see how it is vital that the wheel keeps turning. In this pastoral cycle, we may begin by identifying a practical issue to be addressed, something quite straightforward in our daily life and work; next we seek to develop methods and ways of understanding by which we can address that issue; and then theology may be brought in, to criticize our understanding and our methods in the light of faith, to challenge them or reinforce and strengthen them. But our theology in its turn will be subjected to the criticism of fresh insights and discoveries, both from its own theoretical disciplines of biblical studies, history and the like, and also from our own experience and other kinds of knowledge. The revised theology which results from that will open our eyes to new ways of seeing the world, and make us sensitive to new practical issues to be faced. So the cycle begins again, action and thinking always leading on from one to the other. Yet we never merely return to the place from which we started, for always as we move around the circle we shall have been engaged in new projects of practical discipleship and developed new insights along with them.

There are several different ways in which the details of this cycle may be expressed, but the heart of all of them is the same: we do not first develop our theology as a theory and then find out how to apply it once our theory is complete. Theory and practical experience – to which must also be added, the experience of prayer – are interwoven at every point, each is developed with the other, and in their mutual giving and receiving is found the real and living dynamic of our Christian pilgrimage.

In the chapters which follow, we shall meet both kinds of image of the living wheel. In a not wholly systematic way, these chapters will consider a variety of ways of perceiving and speaking about the resurrection, suggested partly at least by various New Testament authors. These rather theoretical ideas will also be set in relation to our own experience, just as the passion of Jesus was set in the first part of this book in relation to the phases of our human pilgrimage. This can be seen as a kind of contemplative exercise on the resurrection, gazing upon it from this angle and from that without demanding (or even thinking possible) that we reach a consistent theory about it. Yet in the process I hope there may emerge a kind of non-systematic consistency, and above all some sense of the possibility of our entering now into the truth and life of the resurrection of Jesus Christ, which is the burning, living foundation and heart of our faith.

9 · SAINT MARK – *GOD IN MYSTERY*

THERE ARE SOME people who seem to be made for suffering; if there is something which can go wrong with their lives, it will. When we meet such people, it is tempting to see it as in some sense their own responsibility, to look for something in their character or their way of responding to life which makes them particularly liable to get the worst of every situation. Yet this rather natural suspicion really fails to do justice to reality. From time to time, we come across someone who quite invalidates it; someone full of sanity and goodness, whose every step still seems dogged by misfortune or pain; someone in whom perhaps the love of God shines out, for whom again and again life simply goes awry. From time to time we may find for ourselves that our best efforts to do God's will, to give ourselves trustingly and lovingly to God, end not just in hardship (which we have been warned to expect) but in confusion, perplexity and deep disappointment. Looking back afterwards, we may be able to make sense of that experience, to see what God was doing with us all along; but we do not see this at the time. In certain times of testing – if they are real testing – it seems as though what God really does to people is to raise us up in joy and hope, only to dash us to the ground at the next moment.

This was the experience of Abraham when, as the biblical writers so briefly put it, he was put to the test:

> It was by faith that Abraham, when put to the test, offered up Isaac. He offered to sacrifice his only son even though he had yet to receive what had been promised, and he had been told: 'Isaac is the one through whom your name will be carried on.' He was confident that God had the power even to raise the dead; and so, figuratively speaking, he was given back Isaac from the dead.
>
> Hebrews 11.17–19

It was not simply that God demanded the death of his son, terrible though that would have been. More fundamentally, the testing of Abraham consisted in this: that the son whom he was required to sacrifice was the son given by God's promise, the son who was to be his heir, the son with whom God had declared that the covenant would be established. When first he heard the promise of an heir, Abraham thought it was a joke. 'May Ishmael live in your presence!' he said, 'That will be enough!' That would be reasonable, a sensible expectation. But God was not to be limited to the sensible; the impossible would occur, Sarah would conceive, and her son Isaac would be the heir of promise.

But now the same God who insisted on making and fulfilling that irrational promise, the same God who against every possible expectation gave Abraham an heir in his old age, this same God required that heir to be destroyed. Abraham had given his whole trust to this God when he allowed himself to believe that promise against all the odds; having once done that, his die was cast, he had no higher trust to which he now could turn. Once having committed his faith to God, there could be no return. But what kind of God was this as object for his faith, in those dreadful hours before the ram in the thicket was revealed, when he believed that he must kill his son? Trust in God was all there was for him; but how could such a God as this be trusted?

Abraham's story focuses for us the nagging mystery which lies at the heart of any faith in God: the insoluble mystery of pain. Not all the pain in the world is caused by human sin, and not all the trouble in our lives is the result of our own faithlessness. Pain is a fact in the world, and it seems to be so whatever we do or fail to do; for some people, it is this fact of pain which brings them to faith in God. The world is not as it should be, it is not altogether the kind of place our best ideals cry out for it to be; for many it is not that kind of place at all. So we long for there to be some reality somewhere in which – or in whom – our ideals can find their truthfulness. We believe in God and in God's goodness because we cannot ultimately believe in the goodness of the world, or of humanity, or of ourselves, but we have to believe in something if we are to be human at all.

Yet this God in whose goodness we believe is, as we believe, creator of this world in whose goodness we cannot ultimately believe. The same brute fact of pain and evil in the world, which may drive us to put our trust in God because there is no other sure grounding for our trust, causes those who suffer to cry out in protest; it causes some to lose their faith; it is apt to leave us all perplexed and puzzled again and again, unable to understand the mystery of God.

It is this same puzzling mystery which was faced by Mark and the Christian community in which he wrote. They knew that God's Messiah had come, and that Messiah was Jesus. They had heard the witness of those who had walked with him in Galilee and Jerusalem, who had been deeply impressed by his person, his message and his acts. They had heard these witnesses give their testimony that God had raised him from the dead, so vindicating his life and message and confirming that he carried God's authority. They had experienced in their own life the renewal of the Holy Spirit when they had believed this testimony and placed their faith in him as God's Messiah. All this was their basic Christian experience, from which there could be no turning back.

But now, like Abraham, they were being tested. In the first place, there is every indication that Mark's Gospel was written in a situation of persecution. The reign of God which the believers had accepted turned out to have no promise of immediate or easy victory over the powers of evil. In the light of this continuing situation, it could be seen that the Messiah in whom they believed was a surprising, paradoxical object for their faith. He had suffered the most abject and disgraceful death possible under Roman rule, a death reserved for slaves and subject peoples without rights of citizenship. It was a death deliberately intended to dehumanize its victim, leaving him pinned stark naked to a beam of wood to die, like a tattered warning-sign flapping by the roadside. If indeed the ancient tradition is correct which places the writing of Mark's Gospel at Rome itself, all this must have been very prominent in the awareness of the community which put its faith in such a man. For them, the scandal of the cross must have been very great indeed.

To compound the scandal, the testimony in which they had believed had said that it was the leaders of God's own people who had handed him over to the Romans for crucifixion; no acknowledgement of Jesus by those who could have been expected to recognize the Messiah when he came. Even his own disciples had deserted him. What sort of Messiah was this in whom to put their faith?

It has become a commonplace of scholarship to recognize that Mark included in his manner of narrating the events concerning Jesus two interlocking themes by which he approached these questions. One theme was the blindness of the disciples. Time and again, Mark shows the closest companions of Jesus as utterly unperceiving, failing to see the point of all his teaching, and even when they catch a momentary glimpse (as when Simon Peter confesses him as Christ at Caesarea Philippi) immediately afterward slipping back into their usual darkness. Their final betrayal and desertion is simply the last act in a sorry tale of continuing blindness almost unrelieved.

Mark's other well-known theme is the messianic secret. He suggests that Jesus deliberately concealed the fact that he was Messiah from all except his nearest followers. When someone is healed, Jesus orders that person to tell no one. When a devil recognizes him, he rebukes it and commands its silence. He does everything to keep hidden the truth about himself, and it is only finally on the night of his passion, in the high priest's house, that, faced with the direct question 'Are you the Christ?', he gives his answer 'Yes, I am'. Secrecy on the one hand and blindness on the other; ample reasons for the failure of his people to acknowledge him as Messiah and for his disciples' loss of confidence at the critical time.

Yet when all that has been said, where does it really get us? Why should the Messiah deliberately keep his identity a secret, only to reveal it openly in a situation of confrontation after his arrest? Why should he choose such blind, unresponsive men for his apostles? If Mark means these themes of secrecy and blindness as an explanation for the mystery of the Messiah's rejection, they do not really help at all – any more than all the suggested explanations of the mystery of pain have ever probed the heart of that. We should see Mark's themes rather, not as an explanation but as an expression of the mystery of God in Christ. Where God is truly present, God's presence defies straightforward, clear revelation; where God is truly present, human perception is shown up in its weakness. Only in the moment of his trial does God's Messiah show his hand; and the clarity of his answer then, 'Are you the Christ, the Son of the Blessed One?' 'I am', is matched by the clarity of total rejection by those who hear that claim. God's truth is inherently dark, obscure, even unacceptable to human sight.

So Mark gives us a puzzling Messiah, no less mysterious than the God in whom Abraham had put his trust. His last intelligible words before he dies are an enigma in themselves: 'My God,' cries God's Messiah as he shares the pain of God's world, 'my God, why have you forsaken me?'

Nor does Mark show us a resurrection which resolves the mystery. It is the most probable view of the ending of Mark's Gospel that the first eight verses of chapter 16 are the conclusion of that Gospel as he wrote it. Certainly the passage which appears in our Bibles after that was not part of Mark's own composition, and there is no convincing reason to suppose that any verses have been lost and replaced by it. So Mark ended his Gospel with the words, 'for they were afraid'. If this is right, then the only resurrection narrative which he gives us is the story of the empty tomb. Is that any kind of evidence for resurrection? Far from it; consider what actually occurs in Mark's account. The women come to Jesus' tomb to complete the ritual of mourning for their dead master, they are confronted by no body at all to mourn, but only a strange and puzzling message that 'He has risen, he is not here', and they run away in fear.

These women have just lost their lord, their beloved leader and friend, the one to whom they had come to look for assured proclamation of the ways of God, one in whom they have invested their whole lives. This man, who meant so much to them, has been destroyed before their eyes – they were there watching even at the end –

destroyed by the cruel, degrading, disgusting death of crucifixion. They have watched while his chosen apostles have betrayed, denied, deserted him. What anger, what frustration, what sense of loss, what guilt, is all bound up in that? And now they come to the tomb, to make what they can of the only link with him that still is left to them, to care for his dead body; and the body has disappeared.

When people suffer bereavement, there are several indicators which are generally used to warn of the danger of a final lack of resolution, an outcome which is unhealthy and stores up trouble for them in the future. When a dearly loved person dies, in whom someone has invested a great deal of their own identity, that is a danger sign; when the death has been sudden, or violent, traumatic, extremely painful, that is a danger sign; when there have been feelings of guilt or anger associated with it, that is a danger sign. And when the body is not present to be mourned, for grief to be worked through, that in combination with the others is a loud and strident warning that something is likely to go wrong in that person's handling of their loss. Every one of these negative, dangerous factors was present in the case of Jesus.

Contrary to popular supposition, the empty tomb is not (as shown by Mark, at any rate) a proof or even a first sign of the resurrection. It is the last straw which breaks the camel's back, the lowest point of the descending slope of traumatic and fearful loss, the final stage in the horror of the death of Jesus. The women ran away from the tomb saying nothing; for they were afraid.

If the empty tomb says anything to us, it is that it is only when the camel's back is broken that new life begins; only when we go down to the very pit of helplessness and hopelessness that God's help and God's hope become apparent. When we draw back from experiencing our pain to the full, when we take refuge from it and insulate ourselves against it, then we deprive ourselves of God's promise of resurrection. For this promised new life comes only when the last vestige of hope for any naturally positive outcome has been totally stripped away.

So the gospel of resurrection in Mark's hands is of a piece with the mysterious behaviour of Jesus as Messiah, and his perplexing end. To his Christian community which is itself enduring the test of persecution, he offers no easy escape at all. He gives no straightforward answer to the problem about God posed by the experience of all who suffer. He merely confirms the predicament, shows us the act of God in Christ, dark and hidden from beginning to end, and says 'Here is the truth, here is God at work.' The fear with which the women run from the tomb is not simply the natural fear of utter brokenness; it is also holy fear, the awestruck dread of the living presence of God the Mystery. To engage with that mystery, to accept the pain, to trust in God even when God seems to be beyond all trust, to believe in Christ in all his hiddenness; that is the only way open to us if God in Christ has once taken hold of our lives. And perplexing, frightening as that way may be, that is the way by which God's promise can be received.

10 · SAINT MATTHEW – *GOD IN TRIUMPH*

ONE WAY OF summarizing the distinctive emphasis of Matthew is to say that he portrays the end of the road for ancient Israel and its replacement by a new community of faith, united under a renewal of the law of God declared by the new Lawgiver who speaks and acts with God's authority. Jesus teaches with all the authority of the divine Author of the law himself: 'You have heard how it was said to our ancestors . . . But I say this to you' (Matt. 5.21–2; cf. 5.27–8, 31–2, 33–4, 38–9, 43–4). His authority is recognized for example by the centurion whose servant is ill, while the final word of the leaders of Israel concerning him is 'we recall what this impostor said, while he was still alive' (27.63). His very birth is prophesied under a name which conveys the presence of God, 'Immanuel'; and at the end he proclaims that every possible authority is his, and promises his own presence to his disciples.

That presence among his disciples is a recurring theme in Matthew: 'Where two or three meet in my name, I am there among them' (18.20), on the one hand; and 'In so far as you did this to one of the least of these brothers of mine, you did it to me' (25.40) on the other. Within the new community of faith is found the presence of Jesus, who himself conveys with all authority the presence and power of God. Meanwhile the old community, Israel by birth, stands condemned and rejected out of its own mouth: 'The people, every one of them' – that is, the entire solemn assembly of Israel – 'shouted "Let his blood be on us and on our children!"' (27.25).

With that cry, we reach an impasse in our reading of Matthew. What does it mean, and what lies behind it? We know what it has been taken to mean, over centuries of Christian anti-semitism. It is only in our day that the Church has publicly repudiated the ancient idea that by this cry the whole Jewish people for ever became guilty of the murder of Christ. Modern commentators tend to encourage us to see it in more strictly limited, historical terms; as Matthew's way of saying that the destruction of Jerusalem (an event in the quite recent past when he wrote) had been God's punishment of the people for their rejection of the Messiah. But that does not help to connect this Gospel with us. Is there anything in our own experience which can take us beyond the merely historical on the one hand and the unacceptable on the other, and enable us to enter into the world of Matthew, to gain value for ourselves from his account of a people rejected, a new community formed?

I want to suggest a way, which begins by going outside the perspective of Matthew himself, back to the mystery of pain and our human response to it. How do we react to pain, our own or the pain of others, in a world which we believe to be God's? For us, so many of our responses (or at least the responses which we think we ought to make) are conditioned by long Christian experience of the cross and resurrection of Jesus, and reflection on their meaning. But suppose we did not have that experience; suppose we knew God only as Creator of this world in which we find ourselves, how should we think of God then? I suspect that our feelings would be rather mixed. Some of the time, we might respond with gratitude and joy, and with love to answer the wonderful gift of life. Sometimes, the gift would not seem so wonderful, and our true and natural response would be sorrow, bewilderment, fear and even anger. The nature and purposes of God are hidden, we ask for meaning and God does not answer; God's silence may drive us, like Job, into torments of fury.

Then suppose that God does speak; but in speaking, what God does is to demand. God makes an absolute claim for our obedient loyalty; God punishes us again and again for every disloyalty and each disobedience. God insists that we observe the highest standards of personal morality and social integrity. God whose own creation is such a mixture of good and evil, pain and joy, demands unmixed, total goodness of us as the only standard to be accepted. What will our response be to such a God?

This is of course no fantasy which I am creating. The history and faith of the Jewish people in the biblical period reflect just such a situation as I have suggested; always recalling God's acts in the past, always struggling to make sense of the pain of the present, always being told they had fallen away and being recalled to faithful obedience. It is all too easy in such a condition to slip into a vicious circle of bitterness, a devilish parody of the living wheel of faith. We find no clear and definite revelation of God in the world, and yet we need to know God if we are to find meaning in life. So without this knowledge, life becomes meaningless for us, or else we grow anxious and insecure about such meaning as we manage to find in it. But then such insecurity quite naturally leads to fear, and meaninglessness to disillusion. We cannot maintain any real sense of purpose in our life, we cannot find any solid support for hope or grounding for our ideals; and so we come to have no hope and follow no ideals. We stagnate in the present, and perhaps we finally learn to defend the present state of affairs, the *status quo*, as the only security we know; we become afraid of change.

Yet perhaps we are not really content; for somewhere we know that only growth gives life, and stagnation is death; and then our memory of the hopes and ideals which once guided us brings an uneasy sense of guilt. We feel that somehow we ought to be going somewhere after all, yet we are afraid to move, uncertain that there is anywhere to go. So we begin to feel trapped, not only by our present condition itself but also by our very sense that our present condition is not enough. Our ideals and hopes still beckon us, but their beckoning has become a burden, and a source of fear. The more we feel oppressed by our failure to live up to them, the less we are able to move ourselves to remedy that failure; and the more we evade the call of our ideals, the greater becomes that frustrating sense of failure and guilt.

Even goodness in the end becomes ambiguous. The God who is the source of our ideals becomes for us a hateful tyrant, imposing on us a demand which we are not able to keep. How can we really see such a God as good? So the vicious circle begins again, growing more and more desperate with every turn, tighter and tighter like a serpent's coils. Would it be any wonder if our resistance finally broke down, and we hit out at God in anger, frustration and pain? Would it be surprising if, given the chance to destroy such a God, we found ourselves driven, even desiring to take it?

I do not suggest that this is the way that Matthew explicitly saw the Jewish condition. I do suggest that it is a psychologically, humanly plausible way in which we might ourselves see the condition of anyone for whom God was experienced in present reality as Creator and Lawgiver alone. It does seem to square with the way in which, once human beings find themselves at variance with power and authority of any kind, their quarrel has a built-in escalation, and an open explosion is all too likely to be the result. What is quite clear is that, whatever he may have meant to suggest lay behind it, such an open explosion is exactly the way in which Matthew presents the final outcome between Jesus and Israel.

At the point of focus is the trial of Jesus by Pilate. Only Matthew tells us of Pilate's wife's dream warning him of Jesus' innocence; only Matthew has Pilate washing his hands; only Matthew records that terrible answer by the Jews. The message is clear: everyone goes into this with open eyes. Pilate knows the motive of the people – jealousy – and he has the warning from a dream, in pagan eyes a warning from the gods, to confirm his conviction of the mischievousness of the charge. So he declares it to the people, in a way which they can understand; washing the hands in innocence was a Jewish ritual, not a Roman one. And the people with open eyes take responsibility on themselves. 'Let his blood be on us and on our children.' We shall only appreciate the real force of that when we recall that the church for which this Gospel was written was probably largely Jewish in origin, and its writer himself in all likelihood a Jew. The members of such a church could not evade responsibility for the killing of Jesus or shift it onto others, as Pilate had done. None of us can; God's people with open eyes tried in Jesus to do away with God, and if the God of the Jews is our God too, the Creator of the whole world and source of goodness for all humanity, then all humanity is liable to be implicated in such a deed.

Then there is Judas Iscariot. It is Matthew who tells us of his remorse, and his attempt to return the money. 'I have sinned,' he says; 'I have betrayed innocent blood' (27.4). In despair he hangs himself, but the priests gather up the money and use it to buy a burial ground. 'What is that to us?' they say. Innocence and guilt are no concern of theirs, so long as their jealous anger can be fully vented against the one who dared to speak and act with God's authority.

As their anger approaches the final point of its working out, the picture is the same. To the mockery on Calvary recorded by all the first three Gospels, Matthew adds a telling detail. 'He has put his trust in God,' say the leaders of God's people; 'now let God rescue him if he wants him. For he did say, "I am God's son"' (27.43). With fearful accuracy they echo the cynical plotting of the godless against the upright in the Book of Wisdom:

'Let us lay traps for the upright man, since he annoys us
and opposes our way of life,
reproaches us for our sins against the Law,
and accuses us of sins against our upbringing.
He claims to have knowledge of God,
and calls himself a child of the Lord . . .
Let us see if what he says is true,
and test him to see what sort of end he will have.
For if the upright man is God's son, God will help him
and rescue him from the clutches of his enemies.
Let us test him with cruelty and torture,
and thus explore this gentleness of his
and put his patience to the test.
Let us condemn him to a shameful death
since God will rescue him – or so he claims.'

Wisdom 2.12–13, 17–20

That persecution of the upright is no tragic mistake, committed in ignorance. It is a deliberate and cynical attack just because he is upright, just because he claims God as his father. It is the open onslaught of wickedness against goodness because it is good, the explosion of our human guilt and frustration against all that summons us to overcome it.

But at the climax of that explosion, God's triumph begins. As Jesus dies, the earth quakes and the rocks are split, the tombs open and the bodies of many holy people rise from the dead. This is no ordinary earthquake, but the expected signal of the end, the coming of God's kingdom in judgement and power. The resurrection of the dead begins at the moment of evil's apparent victory; human anger has done its worst, and still God is triumphant. A centurion, not one of God's people, indeed one of their enemies, stands guarding the cross, and sees all that happens. Like that earlier centurion who had acknowledged the authority of Jesus to heal his servant, this centurion now recognizes the meaning of these acts of power. 'In truth this man was son of God' (Matt. 27.54). But the leaders of God's people continue in their rebellion, demanding a seal for the tomb lest at the end their destructiveness should be thwarted of its aim. The old community of Israel has reached the end of the road; the very veil of the sanctuary is torn in two from top to bottom, the glory of God's presence has departed from the temple and its guardians, and they are left with only an empty shell.

Now the ambiguity of the world has been resolved. In the passion and death of Jesus, two clear and opposing sides have been revealed. On the one side is wickedness, exposed for what it is; on the other hangs a crucified man, but his death inaugurates the reign of God with power. God is against evil after all, and it is against God that evil directs itself. And the victory is finally with God, with the persecuted, crucified, upright man—with goodness. Nor is it his triumph alone. At the climax of this Gospel, the risen Lord appears to his followers and commissions them by that divine authority which is his, to make new disciples in all the world. The rejection of Messiah by the Jews is not the end; for the summons 'Follow me', with which the ministry of Jesus had begun (cf 4.19), is valid still; and in following him, following the renewed law which he had taught them, his disciples both discover and make real his continuing presence in the world.

This is very close to the notion that Jesus is risen in the life of the Church. But vitally, it is based not on the Church's obedience by itself but on the prior victory of God achieved in Jesus. The problem of God's ambiguity must be resolved, before we ourselves can be the community of the risen life. It is resolved not by any goodwill, obedience or understanding of ours, but through the working out of our human resentment against God, and then after that the discovery that the offer of God's presence is still being made for our acceptance. In our human experience, when a relationship has broken down, when mutual attitudes have become dominated by resentment, jealousy or anger, we may try to convince ourselves that we can remedy the situation by strength of will, by our determination to be good; and yet in general how little real good such determination does. Perhaps we succeed in preventing our resentment from coming into the open, but only at the expense of a coldness and aloofness which show that something is still wrong. Or perhaps we maintain a degree of closeness in the relationship, and think we have our bad feelings under control, only to find them slipping under our guard in some apparently trivial remark, some little piece of spitefulness, through which our true feelings are revealed.

The truth is that it takes honesty to mend a broken relationship; and that is not a comfortable truth when the honest fact is that either one party or both feel hurt and angry and want to hurt the other in return. People sometimes say that an open quarrel clears the air; and certainly it can be that the honest venting of anger is the only way of getting rid of it, and trying to hold it back will only force it out in some other perhaps more destructive way. But quarrels themselves are all too easily destructive; too often the venting of anger leads to further anger in return, the hurt is magnified, and almost unnoticed the breach becomes irreparable and hope for healing is lost. If only there were some way in which that were not so! If only one person's anger and pain could safely be expressed without resulting in a vicious spiral of recrimination! If only the revelation of anger in all its fury could be the last chapter, make an end to the hurt and free us to go forward!

That is exactly the promise in the death and resurrection of Jesus, as shown us by Matthew. Jesus is not destroyed by human anger; and the living Jesus does not upbraid his faithless disciples, does not call down curses on his enemies, does not commission his followers to a vendetta of revenge. He simply commissions them to make disciples; to teach (as he had taught) the law of forgiveness and love. He has accepted the worst onslaught of our anger, and neither he nor his love has been destroyed; that is the triumph of God, that makes possible obedience to his teaching, and that creates the Church as the community of his way, the community in which his presence may be found.

11 · SAINT LUKE – *GOD IN HEALING*

Whatever else may be said about the resurrection of Jesus, the starting point is always that it is the resurrection of the crucified. Hence whatever stance we take for contemplating the resurrection will always reflect the way in which we see the crucifixion. In Mark, we have found an enigma, which the resurrection does nothing to solve; it only affirms that there, in the crucified, God's Messiah is to be found, God's promise is given in the very midst of pain and hopelessness.

In Matthew, we have seen God's triumph over the rebellion of human bitterness. On the cross, that bitterness is simply received, and cosmic events signal the triumph. In the resurrection, the triumph takes shape as the opening of the possibility of a new community of faith, following the renewed law of love and forgiveness.

In Luke, we see Jesus from the cross living out that law of which Matthew has spoken, offering hope to the dying thief and forgiveness to his enemies. These two are linked. To forgive is to give to another the gift of their past, accepted and made acceptable by the act of forgiving. Forgiveness transforms the meaning of that which is past; it is the only way of altering what has now been done. Unforgiven, our guilty past is a burden, a source of disgrace, to be kept hidden away from sight; unforgiven, we try to forget it. But unforgiven, our past enslaves us, holds back our relationships, prevents us from moving on, deprives us of hope. By forgiveness, we restore their past to those who have hurt us, and we give them the gift of their future.

What is needed in me, if I am to forgive? The first critical condition is that I must acknowledge my hurt. Some people have been hurt so much in their lives that they retreat into numbness whenever they are threatened, so that they cannot be touched by any further hurt. That may avoid anger, it may create the illusion of forgiveness; but if forgiveness has to do with the mending of a breach then such absence of feeling is not real forgiveness. It represents not healing a breach but building up walls to keep the breach in safe and manageable form. If I am shut up like this in my own inability to feel hurt, then first I must learn to feel before I can go further. A companion without feeling, and a God without feeling, are an invitation to further violence; they evoke in others a desire to hurt them more, in frustration at the lack of personal response.

But when I am hurt, and know that I am hurt, a further condition of forgiveness seems to be that I must know that the heart of myself is grounded somewhere beyond the hurt which I have suffered. Though really hurt, I must know that I am not simply identical with my hurt, that there is more to me than my pain; for if I am reduced to being simply the victim of hurt and nothing else, my hurt will seek its revenge and the violence will continue. From where can such knowledge come? Not from confidence in my own strength and integrity, my ability to rise above my hurt; that is simply opting for numbness, for unresponsive, unfeeling enclosure within myself, and that brings no healing at all. More positively, the knowledge that I am more than my hurt may come from awareness of some significant relationship giving meaning to my life. Perhaps I know within the hurt that the one who has hurt me really loves me despite the hurting; perhaps there is some other who loves me, on whose love I draw for strength; perhaps it is the love of God in which I find my identity, and that is what can enable me to suffer hurt and yet to be myself.

Then also, forgiveness requires that I come to terms with the reality of the one who has hurt me. I must be able to distinguish between the hurt which has come to me from that person and the person himself or herself; I must be able to see that the one who has hurt me is more than just the inflicter of hurt, just as I am more than just its victim. To see that, I will probably have to learn to see that person as someone who also is hurt; I must understand that person's hurting me as the expression of the hurt which he or she has suffered. Quite possibly, I may have to recognize that it was I who inflicted that hurt, whether I meant to do it or not and whether I had any option or not; that person's hurt at my hands is now being returned to me at theirs. In that case, I must honestly search my own conscience to discover the roots of the hurt, and be ready to own my responsibility in it whether by deliberate act or by carelessness.

Then finally and following from that, if forgiveness is to be real then it must not be that offensive sham which we are liable to use in order to manipulate, to make another person feel guilty, to establish and maintain our ascendancy over them. That is the false forgiving which does not acknowledge our own need of forgiveness, the comfortable, complacent forgiving of the one who is always in the right. True forgiveness is not like that; true forgiveness demands that I recognize myself as being in the same company with the one I forgive, not in a position of moral superiority above that person's head. Forgiveness requires heart-searching honesty in the one who dares to forgive no less than in the one who is forgiven; it is not an easy option for either.

On Calvary, Luke shows us Jesus forgiving his enemies: 'Father, forgive them' (Luke 23.43). His prayer for them comes first from the heart of his own relationship with the Father, and depends upon that relationship; in his hurt he knows that his being is found in the Father, and to the Father he turns as he responds to the hurt which he suffers.

Then secondly, Jesus knows that his persecutors are not simply identical with the hurt which they are inflicting. 'They do not know what they are doing.' They do not consist simply in this hurtful act; there is more to them than this, and so healing and reconciliation are possible.

Finally, it is vital that it is Jesus who makes this prayer for his enemies; for Jesus, especially as portrayed by Luke, is in no way one who sets himself up in moral superiority above other men and women. In this Gospel more even than the others, Jesus is friend of the outcast, companion of the sinful. 'If this man were a prophet,' the Pharisee says when a sinful woman anoints him, 'he would know who this woman is and what sort of person it is who is touching him' (7.39). But that is precisely the point; the forgiveness of Jesus comes from no need to assert himself or distinguish himself from the sinful, as the Pharisee expects him to do. It is the parable of the Pharisee and the publican that forms in Luke the keynote to all Jesus' teaching and life. Not self-justification but the hard way of realism and dependence upon the Father at the centre of life; that is the way which makes true forgiveness possible, and that is the way of Jesus.

At Calvary itself, it may seem that none of the hardness of this way is evident in Luke's portrayal, none of the personal trauma seen in Matthew or Mark at that scene; but that is not (as some have supposed) because Luke makes little of the suffering of Jesus, but because he shows us the heart of his suffering elsewhere. If we read the account of the passion of Jesus as Luke has narrated it, we find a series of incidents where the healing work of Jesus is done. It begins at his arrest, where only in Luke he heals the ear of the high priest's servant, cut off by one of his disciples. From the first onslaught of violence, Jesus responds with love, and brings healing to the situation.

Now, this incident has a kind of foreshadowing, which also Luke alone records. At the end of the Last Supper, there is an enigmatic passage which has always caused consternation to commentators: 'If you have no sword, sell your cloak and buy one.' 'Here are two swords,' the apostles reply; and he responds, 'That is enough!' (22.36, 38). One of those swords was used to cut off the servant's ear; but Jesus reached out, and healed it.

After the arrest, Luke tells us immediately of Peter following into the high priest's house, and denying his master; again he foreshadows this, by expanding and emphasizing Jesus' prediction of Peter's denial with features not found in Mark or in Matthew (cf. 22.31–4). And when the denials are done, and the cock has crowed, 'The Lord turned and looked straight at Peter' (22.61), and that was what moved him to tears. Again, Jesus in his time of suffering acts to bring healing to those who wrong him, the spiritual healing of penitence. Jesus looks beyond his own hurt to Peter, and out of his own hurt he heals him.

The next event which is peculiar to Luke is longer: the whole trial before Herod, which no other evangelist records. At its end, Herod sends Jesus back to Pilate, 'And though Herod and Pilate had been enemies before, they were reconciled that same day' (23.12). Returning again to the Supper we find this also foreshadowed; before the strange dialogue about the swords, before the prediction of Peter's denial, another incident which Luke alone records on that occasion: the apostles quarrel about greatness, but Jesus says to them, 'Among the gentiles it is the kings who lord it over them . . . With you this must not happen' (22.25–6). The gentile kings with their quarrelsome hunger for power; reconciliation even between them, in the persons of Herod and Pilate, is given by the presence of Jesus in suffering.

Three incidents of healing. There are more, leading even beyond the death of Jesus to the witnessing crowds going home 'beating their breasts' (23.48), in a symbol of sorrow or penitence; but Luke has highlighted these three in particular, by a standard literary device of his time. With each act of healing he has coupled a foreshadowing, and the three foreshadowings appear in the opposite order to that of the healings. So foreshadowings and healings between them focus attention on the event which stands at the hinge, the point where foreshadowing turns to fulfilment. That event, where revelation of the need for healing gives way to healing itself, marks the real agony, the trauma and the victory of Jesus in Luke:

> He then left to make his way as usual to the Mount of Olives, with the disciples following. When they reached the place he said to them, 'Pray not to be put to the test.'
>
> Then he withdrew from them, about a stone's throw away, and knelt down and prayed. 'Father,' he said, 'if you are willing, take this cup away from me. Nevertheless, let your will be done, not mine.' Then an angel appeared to him, coming from heaven to give him strength. In his anguish he prayed even more earnestly, and his sweat fell to the ground like great drops of blood.
>
> Luke 22.39–44

That prayer in the garden, with its anguish and sweat 'like great drops of blood' (22.44), is where the real work of Jesus is done, that inner work which will make healing possible. There Jesus carries out the heart-searching which will entitle him to offer true forgiveness; there he works through in himself the way by which he can respond to the approaching hurt with genuine love. His final 'Father, forgive them' is built out of the honesty of that prayer in the garden, 'Father, if you are willing, take this cup away from me'; it is built out of the trust of that prayer, 'Father, let your will be done, not mine'; it is built out of the coming together of that honesty and that trust, and the hard, inner work which makes the connection between them. Once that is done, the agony is over; the rest of the story of Jesus is healing and unshakeable trust to the end.

But really there is no end. In Luke, resurrection flows smoothly out of that which has gone before; it is simply a continuation of the healing already begun. 'Today,' says the dying Jesus to the penitent thief, 'today you will be with me in paradise' (23.43). The new life begins immediately, without a break.

Consider Luke's most substantial and distinctive resurrection story, the journey to Emmaus. For the two disciples at the start of their journey, what meaning was there in all that had happened? No meaning, but only pain and regret, and longing for what might have been: 'Our own hope had been that he would be the one to set Israel free' (24.21). Perhaps they remembered his teaching as they talked along the road, and wished that they had been more faithful to it. But now he was gone, the time was past, it was too late. There was no undoing the thing which was done, and the best they could do was to bury it decently.

There is much that is common to all of us in that experience. As we each go through life, the doors close behind us as we move on; what a wealth of sadness there is in that simple fact. We grow up, we grow wiser (we hope), more able to handle our lives; but as we do so, inevitably we leave something behind. A certain innocence, perhaps, a certain vigour, a certain sunny enthusiasm grows overcast with the clouds of mature responsibility. Or in relation to the world at large, we see parts of the country we once knew destroyed for ever by concrete motorways, the places in which we grew up made unrecognizable, curious ways and customs vanish under the juggernaut march of change. Little wonder that the nostalgia industry thrives.

But our lives do go on, and history does not turn back on itself; it is tomorrow to which we must look, knowing that the past is behind us. Is that a recipe for hope, or for tragedy? For as long as the past simply slips away from us, a lost world of missed opportunities and regrets at achievements half made, tragedy has the last word. To set our faces to the future is a matter of stern necessity, but it cuts us off cruelly from a whole world of our feelings, a great part of ourselves. We can never be whole; for what we were is no more, but the memory of it remains with us as an itching scar, reminding us time and again of that part of ourselves which we have lost.

In just such a condition as this, the two friends on their way to Emmaus found their past beyond all expectation restored. Not in a backward-looking way, to hold them entrapped in nostalgia, but in a way which released them for life in the future. 'Starting with Moses and going through all the prophets' (24.27) their new companion took them back over their history, reshaped and remodelled it, refashioned their personal memory in the context of the memory of all God's dealings with Israel, and gave it back to them whole and full of meaning. There is the culminating act of all those healings which had begun in the garden. The hard, inner work which he had achieved, the meaning which he had found in his suffering, now he communicated to them.

Without that communication of meaning, that healing, forgiving reinterpretation of their past, the risen Jesus was not yet present to them, 'their eyes were prevented from recognizing him' (24.16). But given that meaning, when the trigger-moment arrived, they were ready. At the breaking of the bread, their eyes were opened. His teaching, his actions, his claims, his presence among them, his removal from them, his suffering, his death, all fell into place, and they saw.

Not because they expected to see, not by the cleverness of their own thoughts, but because he had shared his meaning with them, and in that meaning had given them himself. Later, in the Acts of the Apostles, Luke is going to present St Paul's meeting with the risen Christ as a realization of the meaning of his own action in persecuting the Church: 'Saul, Saul, why are you persecuting me? . . . I am Jesus, whom you are persecuting' (Acts 9.4–5). That vision will blind him, but his eyes too will be opened, his sight will be restored at the hands of Ananias, when the Holy Spirit comes on him and he is baptized. So too here in the Gospel, the two friends at Emmaus encounter the risen Jesus through coming to see the meaning of his life and his passion. We cannot ask whether they saw the meaning and therefore believed that he was alive, or whether they were shown that he was alive and therefore perceived his meaning; for his life and his meaning are one, and both are given together. To be shown the meaning, to receive wholeness, forgiveness, healing, is a gift from beyond ourselves. That gift is itself the gift of his risen presence.

12 · SAINT JOHN – *THE VICTORY OF FAILURE*

IN AN EARLIER chapter, we focused on the failure of Jesus: 'We shall never approach the truth of the cross, until we have grasped the profound degree to which it is a failure and a sharing in the frustration of our fallen condition' (p. 15). The Gospel of John presents at first sight a challenge to that way of thinking, for in John we find Jesus always in control of every situation, never a failure even when the opposite seems to be true. In the judgement hall of Pilate, it is Jesus who really puts the governor to the test and not the other way about. Caiaphas' cynical comment 'Better for one man to die for the people' (John 11.50) is, unknown to Caiaphas, a true prophecy of the fulfilment of the purpose with which Jesus himself has come into the world. With his disciples and his enemies alike, Jesus in John seems always one step ahead, anticipating their response before they make it, controlling the progress of every scene, the master of every move as he is the Lord of history.

Did Jesus then fail after all? If we see his death as a failure, is that because we impute to him intentions and hopes which he never had? It is natural enough for us to suppose that in his teaching he tried simply and clearly to proclaim the coming reign of God and to convince those who heard him; but is that in fact what he was attempting to do? What of his speaking in parables, a device which seems to conceal as much of the truth as it reveals? What of the enigma in which he preserved his identity? What of his way of speaking (especially in John) which appears sometimes to be deliberate provocation, designed apparently to antagonize his opponents or even the wavering? Did Jesus really want to convince those who heard him?

Modern scholarship has cast such doubt on the factual accuracy of our knowledge about Jesus that it sometimes seems hard to say anything with certainty about his words or his actions. But one thing does appear to be clear: Jesus set out to proclaim a critical choice for God's people, a choice which could not be avoided. He did more than proclaim it; he concretely offered that choice by means of his own actions, and by parables meant not to instruct but to pose the challenge in ways which his hearers could not avoid. Because of this, their response to him became the touchstone of judgement; their acceptance or rejection of his words, his miracles, his fellowship with sinners was the way by which they made their choice for God or against. A decision for or against Jesus was a decision for or against God and God's Kingdom.

So Jesus appears to have claimed. In one sense, then, on the cross he succeeded; his being rejected was not a failure. He offered the choice, he made the challenge, as he intended to do; the fact that the choice was rejected meant that the whole of God's people was judged. That was their failure, not his.

But here we face a problem. Judgement, says Jesus in John, was not the purpose of his coming: 'I have come not to judge the world, but to save the world' (John 12.47). The historical roots of this lie in the way that Jesus related to those who were rejected. Like the great prophets before him, Jesus did not distance himself from those who were to be judged through him; that was a vital part of the point of his eating and drinking with sinners, his table fellowship with the spiritually hopeless. Like Jeremiah, like the 'suffering servant' in the Book of Isaiah, the prophet Jesus identified himself with his people, even with the erring, sinful people, and their sorrows became his own. So when Israel is condemned in its rejection of him, he does not stand piously on one side, secure in his own godliness and watching their downfall; he is identified to the end with sinners even while he proclaims the judgement upon them.

When his 'hour has come' (17.1) and he dies on the cross, Jesus has set before the people the definitive challenge for God or against. In this he has succeeded only too well. No one at all has met the challenge; and so in his purpose of purifying a people for God, he has left God without a people at all. 'Lead us not into temptation,' we pray, for there are some challenges, some temptations, beyond all our strength, and exposure to them is only too likely to spell disaster for our integrity. Jesus has led the people into just such a temptation. He has compelled them to side with the sheep or the goats; and the result is an empty sheepfold. So in succeeding, he has failed; the agony of that is expressed in his cry from the cross according to Mark and Matthew, 'My God, my God, why have you forsaken me?' It is expressed in the garden agony in Luke. It is expressed equally in John, when from the cross he cries out, 'I thirst!' (19.28).

That cry of thirst in John is no ordinary desire for physical refreshment. This is the thirst of the one who once said, 'No one who drinks the water that I shall give him will ever be thirsty again; the water that I shall give him will become in him a spring of water, welling up for eternal life' (4.14). This is the thirst of the one who has confidently promised the Holy Spirit to his disciples, and has spoken of that Spirit as 'streams of living water' flowing out of a faithful believer's heart

(7.37–9). This is the thirst of the one who took ordinary water and turned it into wine, and who also said to his disciples 'I am the vine, you are the branches' (15.5). For such a one to thirst is for him to suffer the disintegration of his very self, the eclipse of the centre of his being; and the centre of his being is God and God's reign. For Jesus, in his thirst, his mission is no more.

Where does that leave God? All Israel is lost, there is no one to stand with the crucified prophet, and the reign of God is thereby denied. God's reign has not come, for no one has allowed God to reign in his heart. So the very proclamation on which Jesus based his challenge is proved to be false. Whose god is God now? If the meaning of all that God does is love for God's people, as prophets through the centuries have declared, then now when God's people totally reject the one who has offered the challenge to be for God or against, God's cause is lost. 'I thirst' is the cry of God's longing for loss of God's people. Love is defeated, God's heart is broken; and when love is defeated, there is nowhere to go. Sheer force of will cannot restore a broken heart.

Will God then repudiate Jesus? Will God say that this prophet was false in his claim to present the definitive challenge? Will God declare that after all in rejecting Jesus they have not rejected God, that hope still remains for the people? Will God send another prophet, who may succeed where Jesus had failed? If God does that, then God will be declaring that Jesus was wrong about God; that the God whom Jesus proclaimed is not the true God at all. Jesus has totally identified himself with God's purpose of love for God's people, and because of that identification he has been rejected and killed. So the cross marks the end of the road for that God whose purpose Jesus proclaimed. When Jesus is killed, that God has no future, if the true God repudiates Jesus.

Or will God accept Jesus after all? Will God affirm

that this prophet was true, that the challenge which Jesus posed really was the touchstone for accepting or rejecting God's reign? But then we find ourselves no further forward: if that really is the truth about Jesus, then in his rejection all stand condemned; the truth about God is as Jesus taught it, but the people of God has come to the end of the road.

Only one way forward remains. If God can offer a way for God's people to accept Jesus now, whatever was done in the past, then there is still hope; there can still be a people of God, still a community called together by accepting God's challenge presented in Jesus. That is indeed what God offers, when God raises Jesus from the dead. In raising Jesus from the dead, God declares that Jesus was true; and in making known the resurrection of Jesus, God offers a new opportunity to accept the one who had been rejected and killed. The revelation of the risen Lord may take many forms: the continuing presence of the enigma he posed; the community of faith; the discovery of the meaning of his life; the continuation of healing, forgiveness, reconciliation. In John, the revelation is shown in the form of an empty tomb with its grave-clothes, the sound of a voice speaking Mary's name in the garden, the renewal of the offer of peace to frightened disciples, the acceptance of Thomas' doubt, and the reconciliation and commissioning of Peter. None of these forms presents out-and-out proof; all require faith, for all are opportunities given by God to accept the one who had once been rejected, whose rejection had seemed the end of the world.

The resurrection itself is beyond our awareness, hidden in the mystery of God. What comes to our awareness is essentially sacramental, a set of events in this world conveying a real meaning beyond their visible surface. That is the significance of those strange meetings with the risen Lord in John and also in Luke, where Jesus is present but not immediately recognized. The speaking of a name, the giving of peace, the breaking of bread; these are the triggers which spark realization of God's act. His love for the sinful, his offer of community, his table fellowship, are still abroad in the world after all, when the whole world has lost hope by its rejection of him. This is the Holy Spirit which he gives to his disciples, in the very act of revealing himself to them as risen from the dead, the Spirit by which the love of Jesus is still abroad in the world.

So God takes on a new and definitive name: the One who raised Jesus from the dead; or, the One who sends the Holy Spirit (these two are the same). And Jesus himself can be redefined. Not simply, he who speaks God's word (as in Mark); nor simply, he who fulfils God's word (as in Matthew); nor yet simply, he who is sent by God's word (as in Luke); but rather (as in John) he who himself is God's word, the voicing by God of God's purpose and meaning.

Inwardly speaking, in John, Jesus is God's word because of his total identification with God's purpose, his obedience to the Father; this we have seen also in Luke, critically worked out in his prayer in the garden. Outwardly speaking, Jesus is God's word because he does the acts of God, with God's power and authority. These acts include critically the bringing to light of goodness and evil; this we have seen also in Matthew, where the cross is the climax of rebellion against God, and resurrection the commissioning of the community of love. On the level of communication, Jesus is known to be God's word because he is hidden, unbelieved, of unknown origin, the revelation of the God who is Mystery; this we have seen also in Mark, in the enigma of Jesus persisting right to the end.

So John takes themes which the other evangelists have already explored, and weaves them together in a new creation. He gives to these themes an overall transformation, by relating them thoroughly to the whole life of Jesus. For John, the resurrection is a constant reality, permeating the whole presence of Jesus. 'Your brother will rise again,' he says to Martha on the death of Lazarus; 'I know he will rise again, at the resurrection,' she replies. 'I am the resurrection,' says Jesus (11.24–5), and in his presence the dead man rises. Wherever he is, there is the enigmatic but enlightening, life-giving but judging presence of God's offer and challenge. In Mark, the mission of Jesus looks forward to the crisis expected in the future, when all will be made plain at his coming in judgement. In Matthew, the mission of Jesus reaches its crisis with the cross. In Luke, it reaches its crisis in the garden. In John, there is in that sense no crisis at all, for Jesus himself is the crisis for the world. God in Jesus addresses God's word to the world from beginning to end. That is why Jesus is shown as being in control of every situation, every meeting and every relationship in which he is involved. God's word is sure, it cannot fail or be destroyed; but the content of that word, what it is that God is saying in Jesus, is love; and love can weep for the death of a friend, love's heart can be troubled, love can thirst, and die.

We make a mistake if we think that John is writing a treatise, constructing a system; he is not. He is doing something much more elusive than that, which involves his working on different levels at once. When John has Jesus say 'As I have power to lay down my life, so I have power to take it up again' (10.18), he does not mean that Jesus historically said that; he does not even mean that Jesus historically had that power. What he means is that, in the weakness and suffering of the actual passion of Jesus, the true meaning is God's unswerving, victorious purpose of love. God is in control, and God's word here affirms the power of God. But God's control and God's power have only one form, in the visible events of the world; and that form is service, suffering, identification with the sinful, in a word, love.

In the resurrection, we find both power and suffering, continuity and discontinuity. The continuity is the continuity of love, its unshakeable, unchanging purpose. In Luke, the two friends on their way to Emmaus find that the purposes of God have not after all been reversed; they are shown that the recent events in Jerusalem are all of a piece with God's dealings with the people throughout the ages, still part of the same secure promise of love. Their restoration to wholeness by this means is all of a piece with the restorations which Jesus had always brought about. So too in John, it is love that is recognized by those who meet the risen Lord. In the speaking of Mary's name, in the greeting of peace to his frightened disciples, in the patient acceptance of Thomas's frailty, the same love is seen as they had always known; and in the continuity of that love, they recognize their Lord.

The discontinuity comes from the shape which love takes, the price which love pays. Tested to death, love lets itself die. Offering love, and giving himself completely to that offering, when he who loves is rejected, his whole being is destroyed. 'I thirst' says the one who has promised unquenchable springs of living water. If out of that destruction the offer of love is renewed, that can only be described as a miracle, a fresh creation out of the nothingness of failure. In John, the continuity and the discontinuity come together above all when Jesus is 'lifted up' on the cross. This is truly his 'exaltation', the culminating act of obedience and love, the fulfilment of love's constancy. But it is also his 'lifting up' as Moses lifted up the serpent in the desert. That serpent was the image of Israel's sin, by looking on which their sin was healed. So the death of Jesus is the image of our sin; by looking on the cross (which means, by ceasing to claim that we have no sin, by acknowledging our share in the sin which destroyed him) we are moved to penitence, and so receive healing, the healing of forgiveness.

Forgiveness above all is the miraculous event where we meet the resurrection, the event in which the Spirit of Jesus is present. Underlying forgiveness is the constancy of love; that is unchanging, always ready. But the act of forgiveness itself springs out of love's hurting, out of that which by rights should destroy it. In the holding together of the reality of hurt with the constancy of love is found something genuinely new in the world. The final chapter of John, though almost certainly an appendix and not part of the original Gospel, is an apt conclusion in the spirit of the rest. Peter by the lakeside is not allowed to forget his offence; three times his love is questioned, to match his three denials, and the experience causes him pain. Forgiveness is not forgetting, but healthy and healing remembering. As he remembers, he finds that his call is renewed. Wherever that happens, whether it is God's forgiveness we receive, or the forgiveness of others, or whether we find that we ourselves are given power to forgive – and we have been told that all these are connected – there we find resurrection now.

> Love bade me welcome: yet my soul drew back,
> Guilty of dust and sin.
> But quick-eyed Love, observing me grow slack
> From my first entrance in,
> Drew nearer to me, sweetly questioning,
> If I lacked anything.
>
> 'A guest,' I answered, 'worthy to be here.'
> Love said, 'You shall be he.'
> 'I, the unkind, ungrateful? Ah my dear,
> I cannot look on thee.'

Love took my hand, and smiling did reply,
  'Who made the eyes, but I?'

'Truth, Lord, but I have marred them: let my shame
  Go where it doth deserve.'
'And know you not,' says Love, 'who bore the blame?'
  'My dear, then I will serve.'
'You must sit down,' says Love, 'and taste my meat.'
  So I did sit and eat.

George Herbert
from *The Temple*

13 · The Openness of God

The theme of forgiveness, with which we were concerned in relation to Luke and John, made reference to memory and to hope, to healing our past so that we may live for the future. Christians are essentially caught between memory and hope; between the memory of Jesus in history, and hope for his coming in glory. The Apostles' Creed says only this about the work of Christ and the purpose of his life, that 'He will come again to judge the living and the dead.' Paul at Athens in the Acts of the Apostles (cf. Acts 17.30–1) has the same theme: the real work of Christ, for which his resurrection is a public commissioning, is to judge the world and so to do away with all the worship of false gods tolerated among the nations in the past.

The Nicene Creed sets this final work of judgement in a broader context. It is 'for us men and for our salvation' that Jesus was born, 'for our sake' that he was crucified; his whole life and death are now seen as part of the purpose which will be completed when he returns in judgement. But even they are not its beginning; the first part of his work is affirmed in the Nicene Creed, as it is by John and by Paul, as being at the very origin of all things, in the creation of the universe: 'Through him all things were made.' We live between Christ and Christ, between our Creator and our Judge; and it is the same person who came in history as a baby, the same person who taught and healed in Galilee, the same person who was crucified outside Jerusalem, the same person to whom we and all things look for our beginning and our end.

The baby, the teacher and healer, the crucified; and the Creator and Judge of all. The resurrection is that which connects these two, which declares the identity of the one with the other. He who 'in terms of human nature was born a descendant of David,' says Paul, 'in terms of the Spirit and of holiness was designated Son of God in power by resurrection from the dead' (Rom. 1.3–4). Hence we can approach the question 'What do we mean by his resurrection?' by asking what we make of these ancient beliefs in Jesus Christ as Creator and Judge; and that is hardly straightforward.

The end of the world and Christ's coming in judgement have been postponed and failed to materialize for so many centuries that to many they seem a mere figure of speech. Perhaps for most Christians today they do not play much part if any in the daily practice of our faith. Yet for the earliest Christians, their expectation seems to have been at the very heart of faith. In some strands of New Testament writing, indeed, 'Christ is risen' really means 'Christ is exalted, and waiting to come'.

The idea of Christ as Creator is similarly absent from most popular Christianity, which prefers to think in simpler terms of God the Father who created us, Jesus Christ God's Son who died for us, and the Holy Spirit who dwells within us now. Yet for John, for Paul, and for those worshippers of God and teachers, who in the early centuries set out the basic pattern of Christian faith in the Nicene Creed, this too was an essential part of their belief in the fulfilment of God's purpose through Christ.

We can begin by asking about the meaning of that: what is God's purpose for us, the purpose which the scriptural and other early Christian writers see as beginning with creation and reaching completion with judgement, the purpose whose fulfilment the resurrection of Jesus declares through him?

Most simply stated, the purpose of God is that we should be free. But when we say that, we have in saying it posed a vast problem, which is the centre and focus of the whole question of God's work in Christ. God is Creator of the universe; and what God does in creation is to allow something else to be besides God. God is Creator of humanity; and in creating us, God allows someone else to be a person besides God; God allows us to be, and to be free. Yet how is it possible to make people free? How can God – even God, or especially God – make us, and in making us, so make us that we are not our Maker's slaves, but free?

God, we say, is all powerful and all wise. But power is about the exerting of control, and wisdom has a way of imposing its insights on the future. In this world which God has made, wisdom and power determine what shall follow after; and a determined future is really no future at all. A world in which the lines of time go on their predetermined way is a world in which time is not real at all, a world in which what seems to be the movement from past to present and from present to future is really nothing but the unrolling of the fixed, unchanging pattern which was woven into it from the beginning. All is really present, in the omniscient, omnipotent present awareness and power of God.

But let us suppose that the omniscient, omnipotent God really does wish to create a world in which the future is real, a world in which freedom is not an illusion. How can God create a world with a real, free future in it?

Sometimes, there are periods in the world's history when it seems as though the world indeed has no future, when it appears that it does run on predetermined lines and there is no point in trying to change it, or when it appears that the world has gone as far as it can go and has run out of space for any further development. Our own age may from time to time appear like that, in ways which affect all of us and help to govern the basic attitudes by which we live. Do we have a future, this race on this planet, or are we nearing the end of our time? Have we run ourselves into the ground? There have been other times in the past, when for some part at least of humanity it seemed as though either the end had come or else the pinnacle had been reached and there was nowhere else for the world to go; and one such time was the period which we know as the first century AD.

The first century in the world surrounding the Mediterranean Sea was dominated by three determining successes. The first success was the political dominion of Rome; not geographically the largest empire which that world had ever known, but the most single-minded, the best organized, the most powerful force yet seen for reducing all human history to the working out of a single political system. The second success was the philosophy of the Greeks, the most far-reaching, many-sided and profound series of approaches to understanding the reality of our being which the human mind had ever achieved; there are those who believe that, on certain profound issues of basic reality, the Greek philosophers still stand unsurpassed, even today. The third success was the religion of the Jews, the most detailed, thorough and all-encompassing attempt which had ever been known to submit every aspect of human life to the revelation of the will of God as supreme and only Creator, Lawgiver and Judge.

Political life, intellectual life, spiritual life; 'A threefold cord is not quickly broken' (Eccles. 4.12). These three powers between them could set up a force for human domination to cut off the prospect of all future growth at the source. Where could political history go, with the unifying system of the Roman Empire established and steadily expanding its bounds? Where could the history of human thought and understanding go, with the intellectual systems of Plato and Aristotle providing ways of answering all the questions of which anyone could think? Where could human spiritual history go, with the Jewish law offering a system to provide for every eventuality of human life under God? For humanity to have a future, these three powers had to be broken; and broken they were, over that and the succeeding centuries, broken in a process which began with the breaking of the mastery of God.

What God achieved in Jesus was the ironic success of failing to succeed, so leaving us entirely free. God in Christ became subject to us, not in some kind of well-meaning pretence (as a father might in play pretend to be subject to his children, only reserving to himself the all-important right to take back control at the moment of his choice), but in actual, serious and literally deadly earnest. In Jesus Christ, the one who governs all things in heaven and on earth left it to humanity to decide his future. In Christ, the one whose reign on earth is said to be the purpose of all human history surrendered in death all hope of securing that reign.

Except that there is not, and never was, and never can be any hope of 'securing' the reign of God. For the reign of God is freedom, and freedom cannot be secured. All attempts to secure or guarantee the reign of God, all attempts to work to ensure its coming, utterly and irredeemably miss the point. Freedom, the reality of a real future, God's reign, cannot in principle be engineered or ensured. The attempt to ensure its coming is doomed to failure from the start.

So God failed. He did not engineer his failure. Jesus

did not try to be rejected; he tried to proclaim the coming reign of God and to convince those who heard him. He did his best. But he did his best within the limits irrevocably set by his purpose of freedom; and such a best will not, cannot enforce obedience. And so in place of enforced obedience (which could not be obedience to God, whose unchanging purpose is our freedom) he received from humanity the response which he had not wanted, but had no way in heaven or on earth of preventing: the response of free rejection. He tried to win humanity's response by the way of freedom; and in trying it, he failed.

God failed; and at the completion of his failure, at the point of irreversible dissolution of God's purposes into nothingness, the dead body is no more, and God's open future breaks through. In the very act of allowing himself to fail, God in Christ has succeeded in the only way which can be success for God. We are allowed to grow up, no longer slaves but daughters and sons. When their children grow up, human parents (if their love for them is genuine) rejoice at their independence, though in that independence children may cause their parents pain. So God rejoices at our independence, though the supreme act of that independence is to put God to death.

'O happy fault, O necessary sin of Adam, which gained for us so great a Redeemer!' So the mystery is proclaimed in the darkness before the dawn in the ancient liturgy of Easter. Not that God rejoices in sin; of course not that. But in a way which finally can only be called 'mystery', God does rejoice in that use of human freedom of which sin is the strongest evidence. God's triumph is achieved in and through our sin, in and through our failure to obey, our waywardness, our bitterness, our absorption with ourselves. What it means for God to create, that ultimate act of divine wisdom and power, is seen in the powerless, foolish figure of a human being hanging rejected on a cross. That is the purpose, the meaning which makes sense of the world, which entitles us to call the world 'creation', and not a mere accident of chance.

Here too is judgement, the measure against which all our obedience is tested. If this is God, then in the service of such a God only one question will finally matter: are we open in our service to God's own self-effacing openness, or are we too bound up in our own success (whether as God's servants or in any other respect) for us to be able to leave God's future and God's people space to be? That is the difference between life under grace and life under law, the freedom of God and the slavery of sin. With the God whose power is revealed in the ability to take human weakness into himself, the world lies open before us, and we can go anywhere at all. In the hands of this God, we are not slaves; but in the hands of any other god, any other power, any other driving force or motive at all, slaves are just exactly what we are. The resurrection is God's act releasing us from that, God's offer of freedom at the heart of creation. Our response to that offer will be our judge.